MILLIONAIRE MIND SHIFT

CHANGE YOUR THINKING, CHANGE YOUR WORLD

JOHN MCNEILL

Table of Contents

Why Am I Writing This Book?

I'm writing this book because right now our country is faced with unprecedented times of being shut down due to a Global Pandemic. The economists are predicting that this may lead to a recession and possible depression. The stock market has been extremely volatile, and for the armchair traders, millions have been lost. Things are changing daily, and the world we once knew may never be the same. The unemployment rate is higher than the Great Depression of the 1920s. There is one thing that history has shown us, and that is that after an economic downturn, there is always a recovery. My goal is to prepare as many people as possible to capitalize during the recovery stage and create wealth for themselves and generations to come. The future moving forward for us all will be very different, and I believe that only the financially fit will come out on the other side of this as winners. The new economy will consist of the Haves and the Have-Nots, and the middle class will be a thing of the past. In my opinion, everyone should be financially free, by becoming a millionaire, to not be dependent on the fluctuations of the economy. Being a millionaire with multiple streams of income is no longer an option and reserved for the elite of the world. It is now the minimum requirement to live in the future. Wealth creation has never been easier than it is right now. Anybody can do it, and you can do it by starting with very little.

In the midst of all of the uncertainty, I wonder how many households have the financial ability to survive this. How many have the financial wherewithal to weather anything that happens to the economy? How long can the average person sustain their standard of living without their job? The average American lives paycheck to paycheck and has a net worth of $10,000 or less. Most

Americans don't have a savings account, and most are one to two missed paychecks away from financial ruin. I'm writing this book because it is now more important than ever for everyone to gain a solid financial foundation — to the point where working your job is optional. The goal for this book is to create a mind shift, in which creating financial freedom with multiple streams of income is the bare minimum for everyone. Anyone that has the ability to read this book and understand these words can create wealth. One source of income is no longer the standard. My hope is that this book will open your mind to the simple things you can do to create wealth for yourself and experience financial freedom. This isn't a guide to the "lifestyles of the rich and famous," although if that is your goal, the same principles in this book will get you there. I want to be clear that being financially free doesn't mean that you make millions of dollars per year or that you have millions of dollars at your disposal in the bank. You are financially free when you own cash-flowing assets that exceed your monthly living expenses. In most cases, you are a millionaire at this point. My goal is to assist 1,000 people on their journey to financial freedom through the basic principles and mindsets outlined in this book.

So, who is John McNeill? I'm a serial entrepreneur and first-generation millionaire, which means I didn't inherit anything from a rich uncle or parents. I actually did it twice after experiencing a personal economic downturn in my life, similar to what the world is facing at the time of this writing. The second time around, I was able to become a millionaire in less time by learning from my previous mistakes and developing my wealth mindset. There were many tough lessons along the way, and I had to shift my thinking and the way I viewed the creation of wealth. I was always ambitious and pursued success, but I was never actually as successful as I wanted to be because I didn't understand the inner game of wealth. Creating wealth is not so much about how much you make, but more so about what you do with the money after you have earned it. It wasn't until I put the principles that you will learn in this book into action that my financial life made a turn, and I haven't looked back since. Life wasn't always as great for me as it is now. I was once the person that would go from one thing to the next, always on the lookout for what's better or greater—simply a better way of life than what I had experienced up to that point. I've read countless books, bought lots of courses, watched YouTube videos on how to be successful, and everything else you can think of. I encourage you to not believe a word I say. I suggest that because I am speaking from my own personal experience on how to make the Millionaire Mind Shift. None of the ideas and concepts that I share are true or false, right or wrong. They are simply a reflection of my own results and the amazing results of my numerous mentors/coaches.

Having said that, I wholeheartedly believe that if you use the principles in this book, you will totally transform your life. Don't just read this book. I encourage you to test these principles out for yourself. The things that work out for you—continue to do so. Discard whatever does not resonate with you. I'm positive that you will find value in at least one idea in this book, and I hope that you have a transformative experience.

I'm sure you've read other books, listened to audiobooks, gone to seminars, and learned about numerous get-rich systems, whether multi-level marketing, real estate, stocks, or business. But what happened as soon as the ride home from the event? For most, not much! You have a short rush of energy and inspiration until you pull back up to your current reality and find discouragement waiting for you at the door, saying, "I told you it was a scam."

You may call me a little bit biased, but when it comes to money, this could very well be the most important book you ever read financially. In the sense of constructing a solid structure for you to live in, this book is your solid foundation to build your dream home on. I get it. That's a bold statement, but the fact is, this book will fill in the gaps for you between your desire for success and your achievement of success. Those are two totally different worlds that require a skillset — a skillset that anyone can obtain with a little guidance and discipline.

There's finally an answer. The answer is law. It's simple. The answer is the law that we must abide by, just as we abide by the laws of gravity. There is no way around it. It all comes down to one thing: if your "mind" is not "set" on wealth creation, no new technique, nothing you know, and nothing you do will make much of a difference.

This book will reveal to you why some people are destined to be wealthy and others are destined to struggle in life. You will develop a deep understanding of the causes of success, mediocrity, or financial failure and begin your Millionaire Mind Shift. You will understand how influences from your childhood shape our financial outlook and how those influences can lead to detrimental thoughts and habits. Powerful shifts in your thinking will take place, and your mind will shift from the non-supportive ways of thinking to thoughts shared with the financial elite. You will think and succeed, just as the wealthy people do. You will also learn practical, step-by-step strategies for increasing your income and building wealth.

In Part One of this book, we will explain how we are all conditioned to think and act in a particular way when it comes to money. We will outline key strategies for making the Millionaire Mind Shift. In Part Two, we will explore the differences between how wealthy, middle-class, and poor people think, and provide you with the necessary mind shifts that will lead to permanent changes in your financial life.

So, let's get this out of the way . . . What is my experience? Have I always been successful? What end of the spectrum did I come from?

Like most of you reading this, I come from humble beginnings and had a lot of "potential," or so my teachers in school would tell me. I did pretty good in school so I had decent grades. I read 2 to 3 books per month, listened to podcasts and audiobooks, and went to seminars. I really wanted to be successful. In hindsight, I'm not sure if it was for the money, freedom, or just to prove to myself that I was good enough, but I became obsessed with becoming a "success." I started several different businesses in my 20s, each with the dream of making my fortune, but my results looked like a roller coaster at your nearest theme park.

I worked 16-hour days in several different businesses from age 19, after a short time in college. Some were a success, but the profitability wasn't worth the headache, in my opinion, and some were horrible failures. "If I just get into the right business, get on the right track, I'll make my fortune," I'd say to myself. Most of the things I had gotten myself into were not really working, so I was on to the next "shiny object" within a few months, buying course after course and going to seminar after seminar. In most cases, I would wipe out any profit that was made in one business that did actually work by chasing "the next big thing." How come others were succeeding in the exact same business I was in and I was on a financial rollercoaster?

I began doing some very serious, deep soul-searching. I examined my true core and saw that even though I said verbally that I really wanted to be wealthy, deep down inside, I worried non-stop about it. Mostly I was afraid—afraid that I might fail, or worse, succeed and then proceed to lose it all. Then I'd really be a loser with a one-way ticket to Loser Ville. What if I found out I didn't have what it took and I was destined to a life of struggle? Sounds a bit dramatic now, but I would really beat myself up at every bump in the road.

Then, as "luck" would have it, I received some advice from a wealthy business owner who I met when I temporarily got a job at a car dealership after going broke from a failed business venture. As a part of selling, it is important to build rapport. The easiest way to do this is by asking questions. As I'm going through my normal sales routine, I found out that the car buyer owns a chain of stores in the exact same business that I was in. He gave me advice that has stuck with me and changed my life, so I'm passing it on to you: *"If you're not doing as well as you'd like, all that means is there's something you don't know."* I'm sure that some people's ego would've taken over at that point and been offended, and for a second I had to think of my response. My guess was that he told me that because I shared with him that I owned a business, but I was standing on a car lot trying to sell him a car. That didn't make sense. I'm sure he was thinking, "Why aren't you running your business instead of trying to sell me a car?" But being the seasoned businessman that he was, he never asked me that. He continued, "Were you aware that most successful people think along the same lines as each other?"

"No, I had not considered that," I replied.

He then said, "It hasn't exactly been proven by science, but in the grand scheme of things, wealthy people think a certain way and poor people think a totally different way. The rich and poor persons' differences in ways of thinking, in turn, determine their actions. Their actions therefore determine their results." He went on, "If you thought the way wealthy people do and did what wealthy people do, do you believe you could become wealthy, too?"

For a second I was confused because my mind went to, "Fake it until you make it," and I was not interested in that at all. But because I was still trying to sell this guy a car and I felt like he was being sincere in what he was sharing with me, I confidently replied, "Absolutely!"

"Then all you have to do is copy how wealthy people think," he said. I sold him the car and never saw this guy again, but what he said sank in.

Although I had become an avid reader, seminar junkie, and a huge info consumer as far as techniques on how to get rich, I had never thought to study how wealthy people think. We all get to see the television's and movie's best rendition on how rich people "act," but nothing on how rich people "think." With me being the secret nerd that I am, I threw myself wholeheartedly into studying wealthy people and how they think. I consumed everything that I could from the Bible about the mind, the law of attraction, and the inner workings of the mind, but I primarily concentrated on the psychology of wealth creation and success. What I discovered was true: wealthy people really do think differently from poor and even middle-class people. I even had to face the harsh reality that it was my own thoughts that were holding me back from wealth. Through this process, I learned several powerful techniques and strategies to have a Millionaire Mind Shift so I would think in the same ways wealthy people do.

After working for a few more weeks at the car dealership, it was time to put my new-found knowledge and awareness to the test. It was the season for the business that I had done fairly well prior to chasing another business and losing my profit. I began using what I had learned by modeling wealthy people, both in terms of their thinking and their business strategies. The first thing I did was commit to playing to win and growing my success. I made a promise to myself that I would focus in this business until I was a millionaire or more. This was a total 180 from all of my previous efforts at becoming successful because I was short sighted. I would constantly get sidetracked by either another good opportunity in a totally different industry or by something tough happening.

In the past, I would unknowingly believe that what my mind said was the truth. I began challenging my mental approach whenever I began thinking negatively or thinking in counterproductive ways. This was very tough in the beginning because we are all human, and most of what we do and how we function is habitual. Changing a habit takes extreme effort in the beginning, simply because we've conditioned ourselves for so long to function in a certain way. Our mind is our biggest obstacle to achieve the success that we want. I chose not to entertain thoughts that did not empower me toward my vision of success and wealth. I used every one of the Millionaire Mind Shifts you are going to learn in this book. Did it work? You bet it did!

The business was so successful that I opened five stores in two states in two years. I hired coaches to help me grow, and I had several mentors that helped me along the way as well. I then began investing my profits into real estate and businesses, under the guidance of wise counsel. This afforded me the time to travel across the country, going to seminars and meeting other like-minded people. In attending tons of seminars, I noticed something strange: You can have two people sitting next to each other in the same room, learning the exact same principles and strategies. One person will take what is being taught and sky rocket to success, but the person sitting on the other side of you will do what? You guessed it, absolutely nothing. I like to call those people seminar junkies. I can identify them because at one point I unfortunately was one. Those were the people I avoided, because I knew that successful people think a certain way. I was there for a purpose, and in most cases, it didn't matter to me the cost. I knew that even if I only picked up one new idea, my return on investment would be exponential.

That's when it became obvious to me that you can have the greatest tools or techniques in the world, but if you've got a leak in your mindset, you've got a problem. You're going to learn how to make the Millionaire Mind Shift—how to think like the wealthy to get rich!

I often get asked whether my success was as easy and effortless as it seems and will it continue. The short answer is: HAHA, heck no, and absolutely by practicing the exact mind shifts I teach in this book. I have now earned millions in three different industries and am a millionaire. Virtually all of my investments and business ventures seem to work out for me! Although it hasn't always been that way prior to my own personal Millionaire Mind Shift, now it feels like I have super powers. I attract the right opportunities and have the clarity to say "no" to what doesn't fit. I have a super power—a super power that you will have, too, once you learn the Millionaire Mind Shifts and do the work.

> *"Living in the moment means letting
> go of the past and not waiting for the future."*

—Oprah Winfrey

It's important for you to recognize how your old ways of thinking and acting have gotten you to where you are at this moment. This book is not so much about learning first. It's moreso about "unlearning." If you're not really happy and really wealthy, I invite you to consider some possibilities that may not fit into your "box" of what you think is right or even appropriate for you.

As you read about these Millionaire Mind Shifts, I want you to test these concepts out for yourself. I'm going to ask you to trust the ideas you are reading, even though I suggested earlier that you don't believe what I say. Test and prove to yourself if the Millionaire Mind Shifts work or not, not because you know me personally, but because what you've done up to this point has gotten you to where you are. What do you have to lose? Better yet, what do you have to gain?

As a coach, my goal is to train you, inspire you, encourage you, and help you achieve your goals. I'm here to hold you accountable for what you commit to do. I hate to be so in your face about it, but it's my commitment to you. I'm committed to do whatever it takes to move you to the next level in your life. So again, don't get caught up in the use of the word "poor" when we discuss mindsets, if you identify with some of the behaviors described in this book. Keep the big picture in mind and use it as an opportunity to grow as a person. You may feel like you're being ripped apart at times, but my goal is to help you become happy, wealthy, and achieve financial freedom. If you want to move quickly and permanently, let's keep going to the end.

PART ONE

Your Money Mindset

The world that we live in is filled with opposites: yin and yang, in and out, up and down, night and day, and more. For one to exist, its opposite must also exist. Is it possible to have night without day? Nope!

In thinking along those same lines, if there is an "outer" game of money, there must be an "inner" game of money. The outer game of money would include things like investment strategies, money management, and business knowledge. These all have their role in being successful and are essential, but your actual mindset/inner game is equally as important. An analogy would be a dentist and his tools. Having top-of-the-line equipment is imperative, but being a top-notch dentist who masterfully uses those tools is even more critical.

I once heard a saying: "It's not enough to be in the right place at the right time. You have to be the right person in the right place at the right time." This is quite true, and I have lived this fact over and over again.

Self-Assessment

Who are you?

How do you think?

What are your habits?

What are your beliefs?

How well do you relate to others?

How do you really feel about yourself?

How confident are you in yourself?

Do you feel you deserve to be wealthy?

What is your ability to act in spite of fear, worry, inconvenience, and discomfort?

Can you act when you're not in the mood?

Here is a harsh reality for you: Your character, thinking, and beliefs are critical parts of what determines the level of your success.

Why Is Your Money Mindset Important?

I'm sure you've heard of the stories in which the star athlete from college gets a huge multimillion-dollar deal and then loses it all, or when people who have been successful in business go sour and have to sell their New York City penthouse and their Miami yacht. What about the lottery winner who found a way to blow $5 million at the local superstore? Now you know the real underlying cause. To the untrained eye, it looks like a downturn in the economy, plain old bad luck, or an unsuccessful marriage, or whatever. On the inside, it's a whole different ball game. That's why, if you come into a large amount of money when you're not ready for it on the inside, the chances are that you will lose it. Most people think, "If I had more money, I could do more with it." That's hardly the case.

The reality is that most people simply do not have the mindset to create and hold on to a large amount of money and the increased challenges that come along with it. That is the primary reason they don't have much money.

Let's take the earlier example of the lottery winner. Research has shown that regardless of the size of their winnings, a whopping 70 percent of all lottery winners eventually go broke and return to their original financial state — the amount they can comfortably handle.

On the other end of the spectrum, something different occurs for the self-made millionaires. Do a little research and look around at your local self-made millionaires when they lose their money. They usually have it back within a relatively short amount of time. Walt Disney is a great example. While his name is now a brand worth nearly $130 billion, Disney was once a struggling filmmaker. His first film company went bankrupt, but he went on to form a new company, the Disney Brothers Cartoon Studio. Disney came close to bankruptcy again when producing Snow White and the Seven Dwarfs, but he avoided it and grew the company what it is today.

Why does this occur? Because regardless of the fact that some self-made millionaires may lose their money, they never lose the most important ingredient to their success: their millionaire mindset. In the case of Disney, if he were still living, he could never be just a "millionaire." His financial mindset was focused on creating billions, and his legacy has outlived his demise by more than 40 years! The average person's financial mindset is set for generating thousands, not millions, of dollars. Some people's financial mindset is set for generating hundreds, not even thousands. And then there are some whose mindsets are set for below zero. These are the people who purposely fit the criteria for government assistance their entire life.

This may be alarming to read, but the reality is that most people never reach their full potential and are not successful. Being successful takes discipline, and most people are simply not willing to be disciplined in all areas of their life. Research shows that 80 percent of the population in the US will never be financially free in the way they would like to be, and 80 percent will never claim to be truly happy.

The reason is simple and staring us in the face: Most people are asleep at the wheel. They are sheep. They go through life living the same year over and over for 40 years. Then, as a reward for working 40 years, they get to retire and now live on 20 percent of what you scraped by to live on for the last 40 years! They work and think on a superficial level of life that is based only on what they can see and touch. They live strictly in the visible world—the "gotta see it to believe it" type of thinking.

I like to think of life and our mindset as the relation between a tree and its roots. Just as the tree has fruit, our fruit is our results. So, let's suppose we look at the fruits—our results—and we don't like them. What do we tend to do? Most of us will start putting more attention and focus on the fruits. But what is it that creates those fruits in the first place? The seeds and the roots that create the fruit—what's under the ground/our mindset that creates results. The invisible is what creates the visible. So, what does all of this mean? If you want to change your fruits, you will first have to change your roots. If you want to change what is visible, you must first change what is invisible.

In my personal experience, what you cannot see is far more powerful than anything you can see. You are going against the laws of nature when you do not apply this principle in your life. You may or may not agree with this statement, but to the extent that you do not apply this in your life, you must be suffering. What is underground creates what is aboveground, and what is invisible creates what is visible. Because we are all human, we are a part of nature—not above it. Therefore, our lives run smoothly when we align with the laws of nature, which existed before we ever did, and work on our roots. Life is rough when we don't.

Placing your attention on the fruits you have already grown is to no advantage. You cannot change the fruits that are already hanging on the tree, but you can change tomorrow's fruits. In order to do so, you must dig below the ground and strengthen the roots.

The Four Pillars of Balanced Life

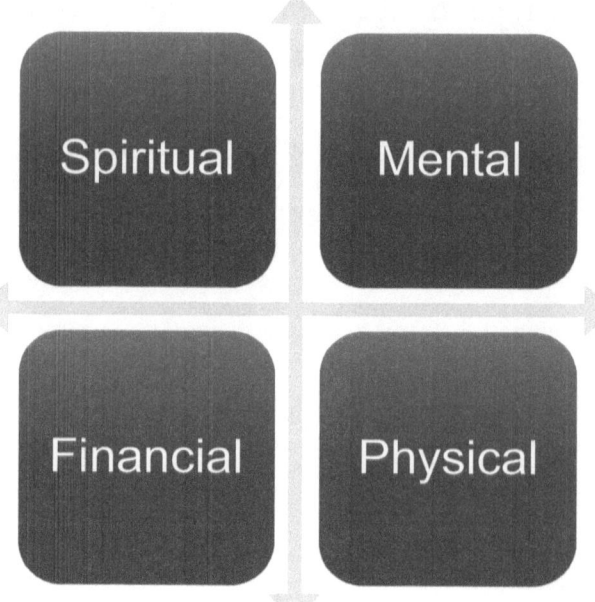

We live in four different realms at once. The four pillars are the Spiritual World, the Mental World, the Financial World, and the Physical World. What most people don't realize is that the physical realm is only a printer, or a mirror, if you will, of the other three.

Here's an example.

You just finished typing out a letter to send to your granny in another state, so you hit print so you can sign it and send it to her. When the letter comes out of the printer, you notice a grammatical error. So, you erase the typo on the printed piece of paper, then you proceed to hit the print button again. When the new copy comes out you notice that the typo is still there. How could this be?

What's going on here is that the real problem cannot be changed in the "printout." It can only be changed in the "program"—the mental, emotional, and spiritual worlds.

We live in a world of cause and effect. Good health is a result, wealth is a result, money is a result, illness is a result.

Most people believe that lack of money is the problem. I'm here to let you know that lack of money is never the problem. A lack of money is a symptom of what is going on underneath. Lack of money is the effect, not the root cause. So, what is the root cause? Simply put: the only way to change your "outer" world is to first change your "inner" world, or your mindset.

Always remember that your outer world is simply a reflection of your mindset. If you are not experiencing good things in your outer life, it's because things are not going well in your inner life. As simple as it sounds, that's it.

Verbalize Your Intentions

I'm going to ask that every time you reach a Millionaire Mind Shift, you commit to verbalizing your intentions. Simply make a positive statement emphatically, out loud. Even if stating something out loud "makes you feel a little weird," I want you to at a minimum think on these Millionaire Mind Shifts throughout your day to see where you can apply your new intentions.

Why is verbalizing your intentions such a powerful tool? When you verbalize your intentions, you send a powerful message to your subconscious mind and God. Some prefer to use "The Universe" or "Higher Power." Please don't get caught up on that part. Fill in the blank with what resonates with you. The difference between verbalizing your intentions and affirmations is very powerful. The definition of an affirmation is "a positive statement asserting that a goal you wish to achieve is already happening." The definition of verbalizing your intentions is "to state your intention to follow a course of action or adopt a certain status."

I've never been crazy about affirmations, because as I state something as if it has already happened, my mental BS meter wails with sirens blazing. It causes me to have conflicting thoughts, like I am lying to myself. With affirmations, you may feel good saying, "I drive a red exotic sports car" but once you go outside of your apartment in the hood and stick the key in your '98 sedan with roll-up windows, all of those good feelings fade away immediately.

On the other hand, verbalizing your intentions is not saying that something is true. You're simply stating that you have an intention of doing or being something. This is a position that will keep your "BS" meter from going crazy, because you're not stating you already have the mansion of your dreams, but again it's an intention for us in the future. In order for this to work, you must take all the actions necessary to make your intention a reality. But you don't want to just take action for action's sake. You should only take action when you are inspired to do so.

Now I have to admit that when I first started learning about all of this, I said, "No way. This verbalizing my intentions thing is pretty weird." I had been introduced to affirmations in the past and did not have much success. But because I had tried everything else, I figured that it couldn't hurt, and I started doing them. Either way, I'd rather be "out there" and really wealthy than really cool and really broke. How about you?

What Is Your Blueprint for Money?

What is your blueprint for money? Use the blueprints for a house as an analogy in the same way your blueprint for money is your preset program in relation to money. The house can't be built any different from the blueprint, just as your financial life can't be built from anything other than your blueprint for money.

I want to introduce you to a formula that many of the most respected teachers in the field of human potential have used as a foundation for their teachings. It determines how you create your reality and wealth. Called the Process of Manifestation, it goes like this:

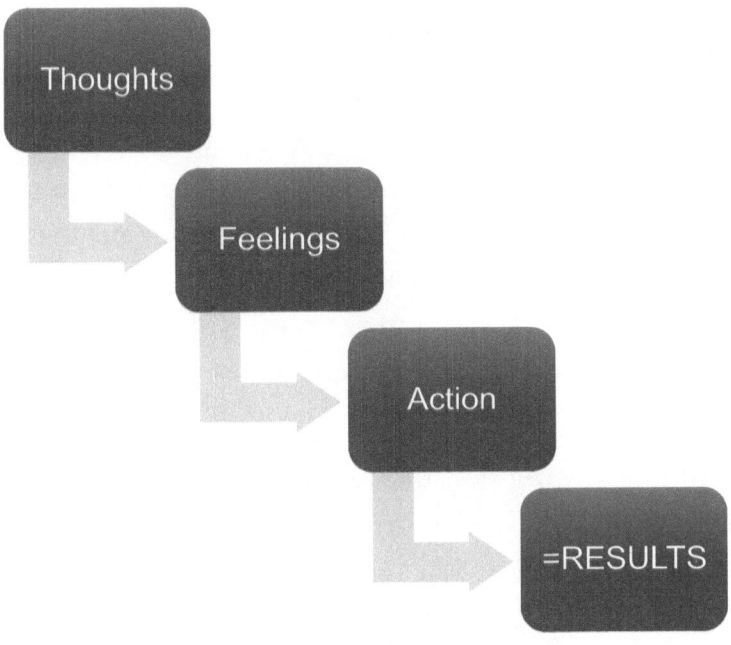

Your financial blueprint consists of your thoughts, feelings, and actions in the arena of money. How is your blueprint for money formed? Your blueprint for money consists of the information you received in the past, and especially as a young child. Some would even refer to your past as "programming." Who were the primary sources who helped you formulate your blueprint for money? For most, it's your parents, siblings, friends, authority figures, teachers, religious leaders, media, the neighborhood you grew up in, and your culture, to name a few.

Isn't it true that certain cultures have a particular way of thinking and dealing with money, while other cultures have a different approach? Do you think a child comes out of its mother's womb with his or her attitudes toward money? Or do you believe that a child is taught how to deal with money? Every single child is taught how to think about and act in relation to money.

There is no difference for you, for me, for everyone. We were all taught how to think and act when it comes to money. These teachings, whether intentional or not, become our conditioning, which in turn becomes automatic responses that run you for the rest of your life. That is, of course, unless you intentionally have a Millionaire Mind Shift. This is exactly what we are going to do in this book.

With the understanding that thoughts lead to feelings, feelings lead to actions, and actions lead to results . . . here's a question: Where do your thoughts come from? Why do you think differently than the next person? Your thoughts originate from all of your past conditioning that you have stored in the cabinets of your mind. Your past conditioning determines every thought that bubbles up in your brain.

We can now revise our Process of Manifestation:

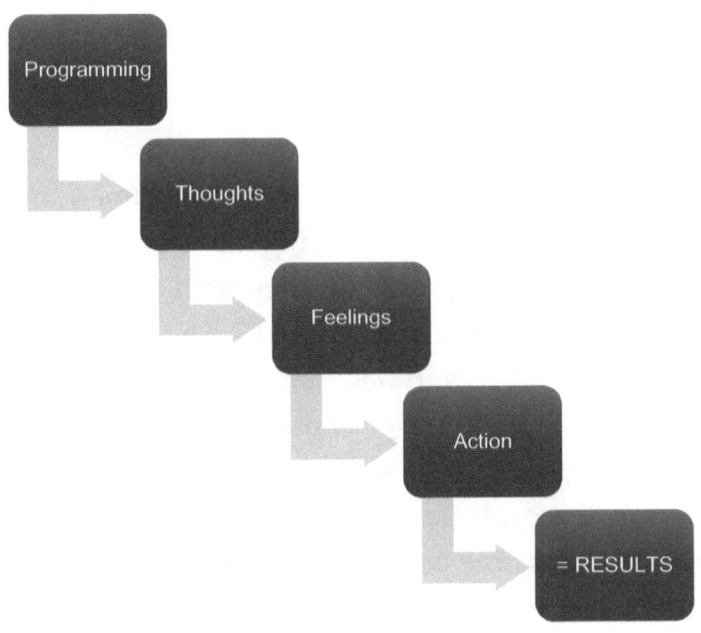

Your programming leads to your thoughts, thoughts lead to feelings, feelings lead to actions, actions lead to results.

We are conditioned in three primary ways in every area of life, including money:

Modeling: What did you see growing up?

Incidents: What did you experience growing up?

Verbal: What did you hear growing up?

These three aspects of your programming are extremely important to understand, so we'll take a deep dive into each of them. In Part Two of this book, you will learn how to make the Millionaire Mind Shift for wealth and success.

Modeling: What Did You See Growing Up?

The first aspect of our lives we are programmed by is called modeling. What did you see growing up from your parents or guardians in regards to money? Did they both manage their money well? Did one manage the money well? Did you grow up in a single-parent home and see money being managed well? Did they mismanage it? Was there never enough to go around? Were they big spenders or penny pinchers? Were they investors or non-investors? Was there always money available for whatever was needed? Did money come easily in your family, or was it always a struggle? Was money the subject of every argument? Were they risk takers or more risk-averse?

I'm sure you're starting to see how these questions are important. Ever heard the saying, "Monkey see monkey do"? Well, that is exactly what happens as kids. We learn just about everything from modeling. For those who have toddlers right now or have ever been around one, you've probably witnessed a toddler repeating the four-letter word you wouldn't want them saying during church service. This is only the beginning, because as we developed in age, we picked up on every single thing we saw growing up—from money to every aspect of our lives.

I'm reminded of another age old saying that we all love, which helps drive this point home: "The apple doesn't fall far from the tree." We've all been to a family function, and out of the blue you will have an uncle or aunt say, "You act just like your dad, smile and all," or some other similar comparison. Although most of us would hate to admit it, they are usually right, and it's something that's inevitable. The point is that, generally speaking, we tend to be identical to one or a combination of our parents in regards to money.

For example, my dad worked for the government. He worked in the mail distribution center as a mid-level manager my entire childhood. His job was salaried, so he was required to work early in the morning until early evening, and sometimes he would have to cover other shifts when someone would call in. Needless to say, he worked a lot of hours, and when he wasn't working, he was sleeping to prepare for the next work day. He was heavily involved in our local church as a deacon and he taught Sunday School, which put even more of a strain on his time. Also, not to mention, I have four siblings and my mother was a stay-at-home mom.

As you can imagine, during my childhood, funds were always tight (or so we were told all the time) With four of the five kids all being pretty close in age, there was always something at school or at church that needed to be paid for one of us. In my household, my dad worked so much, my mom was the wallet enforcer, so if we needed anything, we all knew to go to mom. My parents were savers, so if we didn't "need it," it most likely wasn't going to happen. They were always "saving for a rainy day." There would always seem to be an event that would come along and either completely wipe out their savings or cause a huge hit. If I asked her for anything that wasn't a "necessity," her standard response was, "You better get to work so you can pay for it, because we don't have it." Of course, as a 9-year-old, there weren't many companies willing to break child labor laws to provide me with employment, but my neighbors sure didn't mind! My brothers and I would cut the neighbors' yards to make extra money. As I got a little older, I started selling candy and chips at school, too. I had adopted my dad's insane work ethic and began working as much as I could to earn money, save, and be tight with it, just like my parents were.

Side Note: Saving for a rainy day might sound like a good idea, but it can create big problems. If you are saving your money for a rainy day, what are you going to get? Rainy days, of course! Stop it. Instead of saving for a rainy day, focus on saving for the day you win your financial freedom.

This pattern lasted from the time I could remember, when I was about 9 years old, until the age of 18, when I moved out of my parents' house to go to college. When I went to college, I lasted about four months before I couldn't take the agony of just being a student and not working. So, you guessed it, I got a job. I worked and was busy all the time until I decided that college wasn't for me about a year later. I decided to take on two jobs with no days off. For some strange reason, no matter how many hours and days I worked, I never really got ahead. Sure, I had savings, and I lived on a very tight budget, but there would always be an event that would wipe it all away. This up-and-down pattern went on for a few years as I quit my job and went into several different businesses for myself.

I would start a business, make a small fortune, and eventually be broke. I'd get into another business and feel like I was on top again, only to have a setback shortly thereafter. This pattern lasted about six years until I had an epiphany one day: Maybe the problem wasn't the type of business I was choosing, the partners, the clients, the employees, the economy, or my decision to blow $10,000 on a vacation to relax because things are going well. I finally realized that I was unconsciously reliving my parents' "save and deplete" savings pattern.

Thank goodness I learned what you're learning in this book and was able to shift my thinking to wealth and success, as oppose to the "rainy day" method. Even to this day, the urge to save for that rainy day and to be on a really tight budget (and to sabotage myself in the process) still comes up. The difference is now, when it comes up, I make the decision to dismiss the idea. I now save for my investments that provide me with financial freedom. You can have all the knowledge and skills in the world, but if your mind isn't set for success, you're financially doomed.

Where some people tend to be the identical to one or both parents in regards to money, there's also the other side of the coin. Some of us end up being the exact opposite of one or both parents. How could this happen? Anger and rebellion, anyone? At the end of the day, it depends on how you felt growing up when witnessing your modeling. What this usually looks or sound like is: "I hate you. I'll never be like you," or "When I grow up I'm going to be rich, then nobody can tell me no." Then we run to our room and say a bunch of four-letter words in the mirror with tears rolling down our face.

In most cases, many people who come from poor families become extremely angry and rebellious about it. They often set out to get really rich, and in most cases, they will. But there will be one huge bump in the road. When they do manage to get rich, they are usually not happy. Why? The root of their wealth is anger and resentment, that's why. You just can't make a positive out of a negative emotion. Consequently, money and anger become linked in their minds. The more money this person has or strives for, the angrier they get.

Eventually, the person will subconsciously get tired of being angry and stressed out. The mind answers, "If you want to get rid of your anger, you're going to have to get rid of your money." So that's exactly what they do. They subconsciously get rid of their money by overspending, making poor investment decisions, or sabotaging their success in some other way. Are they happy now? Of course not! Things are even worse now that they're not just angry — now they're broke and angry. Clearly, they got rid of the wrong thing!

They should've gotten rid of the anger instead of the money. They got rid of the fruit (money) instead of anger (the root). Meanwhile, the real issue is and always has been the built-up anger between them and one or both of their parents. Until the anger is resolved, this person will never experience true happiness and peace, regardless of the commas in their bank account.

Your drive, or the motivation you have for making money and creating success, is imperative. If your motivation for acquiring money comes from a non-supportive or negative root such as anger, fear, or the need to prove yourself, no amount of money will ever bring you happiness.

Millionaire Thought

If your motivation for acquiring money comes from a non-supportive or negative root such as anger, fear, or the need to prove yourself, no amount of money will ever bring you happiness.

These are all issues that cannot be solved with money. Using fear as an example, if you were to ask a group of 100 random people, "How many would agree that security is one of the main motivators for success?" everyone in the room would put their hands up without a doubt. Read this twice: Security and fear are both motivated by the same thing. Seeking security comes from insecurity, which is based in fear. So, will more money make the fear disappear? I'm sure you're hoping so! But the answer is absolutely not. Why? Because money is not the root of the problem. Fear is the root of the problem. To make matters worse, fear is more than just a problem. Fear is habitual, and habits can be tough to break without being extremely intentional about change.

Making more money will only change the kind of fear you have. When you are broke, you are afraid of not being able to make it or have enough. Once we make it, that fear shifts to: "What if I lose what I've made?" or "Everybody is going to have their hand out," "Taxes are going to be the cause of my downfall," or "Maybe I should add XYZ to my portfolio just in case ABC goes down." At the end of the day, until we take care of the root issue and eliminate the fear, no amount of money will help.

Don't get me wrong, I know you're thinking, "I'd much rather worry about having money and losing it than to not have money at all," but neither is the way we were intended to live. If given a choice, we wouldn't pick the latter.

Then you have the people who are motivated to achieve wealth or financial success to prove they are "good enough." No amount of money will ever make you good enough. Money can't make you something that you already are. Just as with fear, the "prove yourself" issue becomes your habitual way of living. You don't even recognize that it has completely taken control of your life. For people who are driven to prove they are good enough, it doesn't matter how many commas are in their bank accounts. Nothing eases that inner wound — that inner wound that makes everything in their life "not enough." No amount of money, or anything else for that matter, will ever be enough for people who feel they are not good enough.

Always keep in mind that it's all about you. Your outer world is only a reflection of what's going on in your inner world. If deep down inside you believe you are not enough, you will attract situations to validate that belief and make that your reality. On the other hand, if you believe you have everything you need and that you are more than enough, you will attract situations to validate that belief and create abundance. Why? Well, "everything/enough" will be your root, which will become your natural way of being.

When you disconnect your money motivation from fear, anger, and the need to prove yourself, you leave an opening for new connections to be made to money that well serve you better. You can connect earning your money through purpose, joy, and charity. That way you will never have to get rid of your money to find happiness.

There are four key components of change. Each aspect is equally important in reprogramming your financial blueprint. They may seem quite simple, but they are extremely powerful.

The first component of change is awareness. It's quite difficult to change something unless you know it exists.

The second component of change is understanding. When you understand where your way of thinking originates, there is an opportunity to recognize that it has to come from outside you.

The third component of change is disassociation. Once you come to the realization that this way of thinking isn't you, you can then begin to separate yourself from it. You have the option to choose in the present whether you want to keep it or let it go. You make this decision based on who you are today and where you want to be tomorrow. You can objectively see this way of thinking and see it for exactly what it is—unsupportive information that was stored in your mind a long time ago and may not hold any truth or value for you today.

Millionaire Mind Shift Action Items:

Modeling

Awareness: Take time to reflect on the actions and habits of each of your parents in regards to money and wealth. Write down your similarities and differences to either of them.

Understanding: Write down how this has affected your financial situation.

Disassociation: This isn't you; this is only what you learned. Can you see that you have a choice to be different?

Millionaire Mind Shift: Make the choice to disconnect from any non-supportive habits you were modeled after in regards to money.

Incidents: What Did You Experience Growing Up?

The second aspect of our lives we are programmed by is specific incidents. What did you experience growing up in regards to money, wealth, and rich people? These experiences are more important than you may realize, because they shape the beliefs that you now live by, or better yet, the illusion that you live by now.

For illustration purposes, let's say that Lisa is a successful civil attorney with an excellent income, but somehow, she always spent all of her money and required a "bail out" financially. She would often borrow from the very people she had loaned money to in the past just to cover her bills some months. After reading this book, Lisa realized that as a child she witnessed her parents argue about money after dinner when all of the kids were put to bed. There was a specific incident Lisa remembered, when the usual after-dinner money argument occurred, but this time it was different. This argument ended abruptly with a loud thud on the floor, before her dad had made his first five points. Lisa's dad was dead. He had a heart attack in the middle of an argument about finances.

From that day forward, Lisa's mind associated money with pain. It's no surprise that as an adult, she would subconsciously get rid of all of her money in an effort to get rid of her pain. It's interesting to note that she became a civil trial attorney. Why? Is it possible that she went into a high-paying field to avoid having arguments about money? Once Lisa identified her old money blueprint and made the effort to make the Millionaire Mind Shift, she was well on her way to becoming financially free.

Here's another example of an incident that's a bit closer to home. When my wife was young, anytime she wanted some new toy or to go somewhere that was fun, she would ask her mom. Her mom's response was, "No, you'd better ask your daddy for that." My wife would then call her dad, and her dad would give her whatever she asked for and more! This cycle repeated itself until my wife was 10 years old, when her dad passed away unexpectedly. So, what did my wife learn about money?

First, that men have all the money. Once we got married, what do you think was expected from me? You guessed it—money! She wasn't asking for small things, either. She had advanced to items that cost four to five figures!

She also learned that women don't have money. If her mom (the beautiful wonderful soul) didn't have money, obviously, this is the way she should be as well. Right? In my wife's quest to validate that way of being, when we were dating, she would subconsciously get rid of all of her money. It would almost seem methodical how she could spend every single penny that you gave her. If you gave her $500, she'd spend $500. If you gave her $100, she'd spend $100. Sometimes she would even use the power of leverage and spend $1,000 when I gave her $500 by putting it on a credit card! I tried to explain to her, "If I give you $500, you should spend $250 and save the other $250 for an investment later on."

One of the main subjects couples disagree about is money. We were no different. What we didn't know in the beginning of our relationship was that our understandings of money were polar opposites. I grew up with the belief that money is to be saved for a rainy day. My wife, on the other hand, grew up with the belief that money meant immediate pleasure or expenditure on necessities.

If you could get on the inside of my brain at this junction in our relationship, whenever my wife spent money, she wasn't just spending money. She was spending money that we could've been saving for that proverbial rainy day. As far as my wife was concerned, whenever I held back from spending, I was taking away affection and love for her. Thank God, we learned to have the Millionaire Mind Shift to revise how we act in regards to money. We created a new money blueprint specifically created for our relationship.

A national survey taken in 2017 by the American Psychological Association revealed that 40 to 50 percent of couples name money as the cause of the breakup. As you can see from what we've learned so far, the biggest reason behind the fights people have about money is not in the money in itself. The fights can moreso be attributed to the mismatch of their past experiences in regard to money. It doesn't matter how much or how little money you have. If your money blueprint doesn't match that of the person you're dealing with, there will always be a challenge until these beliefs are addressed individually and collectively. This isn't just for married couples. This also goes for dating couples, family relationships, and even business associates. The key to this is to come to the realization that you are dealing with blueprints, not money. Once you have this lightbulb moment and can identify a person's money blueprint, you can then deal with them in an amicable way that works for the both of you. You can begin by becoming aware that your partner's money blueprint is probably not the same as yours (remember, opposites attract). Instead of looking at the difference as a reason to dissolve the relationship, choose to learn more. Try your best to find out what is important to your partner in regards to money, and identify what motivates and triggers fear. By approaching the situation in this manner, you will be dealing with the roots instead of the fruits.

One of the most important things you can learn is how to identify your partner's money blueprint as well as how to create a brand-new blueprint that helps you, as partners, get what you both truly want. It's a great accomplishment to be able to do this, because it alleviates one of the biggest causes of pain for most people.

Millionaire Mind Shift Action Items:

Incidents

Discuss the history each of you brings to your thoughts about money with the following questions:

1. What did you hear about money when you were young? What was modeled? What incidents occurred?
2. What does money really mean to you? Is it freedom? Is it power? Is it security? Is it status? Is it pleasure?
3. What do we want today as a partnership?
4. Decide and agree on general goals and attitudes in regards to money and success. Make a list and write them down. Post these new guidelines somewhere, and if there is ever an issue, gently remind each other what you decided together when you were both objective.

Awareness: Take time to reflect on a specific incident you experienced in regards to money and wealth when you were young.

Understanding: Write down the emotions that you recall surrounding this incident and explain how this may have affected your current financial life.

Disassociation: Are you able to see how this way of being is simply what you learned and isn't necessarily you? You have a choice in the present moment to be different.

Millionaire Mind Shift: My past experiences in regards to money will no longer dictate my new, wealthy future.

Verbal: What Did You Hear Growing Up?

The third aspect of our lives we are programmed by is what we heard growing up in regards to money, wealth creation, and rich people. Do any of the following sound familiar? You can probably fill in the blank!

➤ Save for a rainy _____.

➤ A penny saved is a penny _____.

➤ _____ is the root of all evil.

➤ You have to work _____ to make money.

➤ Money doesn't buy _____.

➤ _____ talks and BS walks.

➤ The rich get_____ and the poor get _____.

➤ _____ doesn't grow on trees.

➤ They're doing something _____ to make all of that money.

➤ _____ people are greedy.

Growing up, my mom was a stay-at-home mom, so she was basically the COO and CFO of our house. Every time I asked my mom for any money, I'd hear her say, "We can't afford it." I would often mumble under my breath, "I'm never going to do my kids like this. We can't have anything." I'm pretty sure that if she ever heard me, I probably wouldn't be writing this book right now. The point is that all of the statements we heard about money when we were young remain in our subconscious mind today as part of the blueprint that is running our financial decisions.

Verbal conditioning is one of the most powerful aspects of our programming. For example, if you grew up in the 90s or early 2000s, you undoubtedly remember the old milk commercials: "Milk — it does the body good." This was a commercial that ran for many years, promoting the consumption of milk for young kids to grow and have strong bones. As a young child, I was a lot bigger than my siblings and other kids around my age, so my growth was attributed to my overindulgence in milk consumption. Despite the fact that I had the worst stomachaches for the first few hours each day while at school, we ate cereal just about every day for breakfast. Years had passed before my parents realized that I was lactose intolerant, which means that my body had lactose malabsorption.

Side Note: Sixty-eight percent of the world's population is lactose intolerant. It goes beyond the scope of this book, but I encourage you to do a little research on dairy consumption and how we were all duped into drinking milk, expecting it to make us grow stronger. (It actually does the opposite.)

Another example of the power of verbal conditioning came by way of a manager I worked with at a car dealership. Jeff didn't have a problem earning money. He was always faced with the challenge of keeping it. At the time when I knew him, he was earning more than $350,000 per year and had been doing so for the past five years. However, Jeff was still barely scraping by bumming cigarettes from the sales people in exchange for first dibs on referrals. Jeff always somehow managed to spend his money, lend it, or make a poor investment decision and lose it all. Regardless of the reason, his net worth was zero!

Jeff revealed to me that when he was growing up, his mom would always say, "If you have the money to buy it, then buy it. You can't spend it when you're dead." Can you see what was going on inside Jeff's subconscious mind? No wonder he was highly paid and still broke. He was verbally conditioned by his mother to believe that money is meant to be spent as quickly as you get it. After all, you can't spend it when you're dead! Therefore, his mind linked getting rid of all of his money with the point of making money. Because Jeff loves his mom, he can't go against what his mother taught him, right?

You would think that if someone was given the option to choose between being rich and being approved by someone else, most people would take being rich. Not the case! Unfortunately for us, the mind just doesn't work that way. Of course, riches would be the logical choice, but when our subconscious mind must choose between deeply rooted emotions and logic, emotions will be the victor.

In my own life, after several failed businesses, I finally began to do well. However, I never seemed to have any success at reinvesting the earnings into passive investments. Once I became aware of my money blueprint, I recalled in my childhood how my parents would meet with a financial planner/insurance guy at our home. My bedroom was next to my parents' room, so I would often get the inside scoop on the "inside family business." I recall hearing my parents talk about how they aren't making any money with the small investments they had made. My dad would then say you have a better chance of just saving as much as you can and working hard.

Now that you understand the power of verbal programming, can you see why it's obvious I couldn't invest any money and get a return? I was programmed to fail by either hesitating when I should make an investment, not investing at all, or saving in lieu of investing. Why? I was subconsciously trying to validate my money blueprint that said, "You have a better chance at saving than investing!"

It may seem strange, but when you begin to understand how the money blueprint works, it makes all the sense in the world. All I can say is that once I had this awakening, my world changed for the better. It wasn't an immediate change, because I had been that way for so long, but with a little persistence, I began to invest my money successfully. A short while later, my passive investments began to boom. I've had continued, amazing success with investing in other businesses, real estate, and the stock market ever since.

I'll say it again: Your subconscious mind determines the way you consciously think. The way you think determines your decisions, and your decisions determine your actions. Your actions ultimately determine your results.

Millionaire Mind Shift Action Items:

Verbal

Awareness: Take time to reflect on all the statements you heard about money, wealth creation, and rich people when growing up.

Understanding: Write down your thoughts on how these statements have affected your financial life so far.

Disassociation: Are you able to see how these thoughts only reflect what you learned and are not part of who you are today? Can you see that you have a choice in the present moment?

Millionaire Mind Shift: What we heard about money growing up was the way of others. I choose new ways of thinking in the present moment.

The Million-Dollar Question

What is your current money blueprint set for? I know that's the question we've all been waiting on. What result is your money blueprint subconsciously moving you toward? Are you set for a life of success, failure, or mediocrity? Are you programmed to struggle or for money to flow to you easily and effortlessly? Is your blueprint set for hard work and no days off or working in balance?

Are you programmed for having consistent income or a "roller coaster" of an income? You know, the age-old, up-and-down routine we're all too familiar with: "First you have it, but then you don't. Then all of a sudden you get it all back, only to lose it again." Up until now, I'm sure you attributed the drastic fluctuations coming from outside forces. For instance: "I got a high-paid salary position, but the company restructured the executive board and eliminated my position," or "I got another job that was half the pay, but it allowed me time to start a business on the side to supplement income. The side business is booming, but the market dried up," or "I got another high-paying position, but my boss hates me and has it out for me," etc. Don't be fooled for one second—this is undoubtedly your blueprint at work.

Are you aware that there are actual dollar amounts each of us are programmed to earn? Are you set for high income, moderate income, or low income? Are you set for earning $100,000 per year or $1,000,000 per year? Are you set for earning $20,000 per year or $200,000 per year? $75,000 per year or $750,000? $60,000 to $80,000?

The actual amount doesn't matter. What matters the most is whether you are reaching your full potential. We are each individuals and we have our own desires, so one person's full potential may be $50,000 per year while another individual may be currently earning $50,000 per year, but at their full potential could easily do $50,000 per week. I know someone may be asking, "Why on earth would anyone need that much money?" First, that question in itself is a sure sign that you'll want to revise your money blueprint. Secondly, think for a moment how much good can be done by a person that earns $50,000 per week. How much can this person donate to their favorite charity? How much money can this person donate to their local church and put toward changing lives?

As an example, when I first started selling cars, my goal was to simply break the six-figure mark in a year. In my mind, that was the Holy Grail, because no one in my family had earned six figures in one year. I was happy with that amount. I would act out my money blueprint: Earn six figures, save some, then spend the rest. It wasn't until I met my third mentor when asked me why wasn't I earning more that I realized I didn't have a reason. He asked, "Why aren't you earning six figures per month? Why are you 'stuck' at only six figures per year?" Obviously, I wasn't reaching my full potential at six figures per year, but up until that point, I didn't see anything wrong with it. Thank God for my mentor, who helped me to reprogram my thinking and reset my money blueprint for millions.

Are you set for picking winning investments or losing investments? You might wonder, "What does this have to do with whether I make money in the stock market or in real estate?" The answer is simple. You pick the stocks or the property. Who picks when you buy it? Ding, ding, ding! You do. Who picks when you sell it? Again, you do. I guess that means you've got a little something to do with the equation.

I have a friend that is a high-level business owner and investor. He seems to have the Midas Touch. Every business or investment he gets involved with does phenomenal in all aspects of the word. On the other hand, I have another friend who lives in the same neighborhood that I grew up in, who seems to have the kiss-of-death syndrome. Both the Midas Touch and the kiss-of-death syndrome are nothing more than the manifestations of money blueprints. When I asked my friend who's the high-level business owner if he was always like that, because I had only known him a few years at that point, his response was a laugh and, "I wish. I'd be a billionaire by now if so." It's no doubt in my mind that he will be a billionaire at some point.

Not only will your money blueprint determine your financial life, but it will also determine your personal life as well. If you are a man whose money blueprint is set for low, chances are you will attract a woman who is a spender. This will help you stay in your financial comfort zone and validate your blueprint when she spends all of your money. The same goes for a woman whose money blueprint is set for low; chances are you will attract a man who is set for the same.

Most people are under the impression that their financial success, whether from a job or a business, is primarily dependent on their business skills and knowledge. I hate to be the bearer of bad news, but your financial success is only the fruit.

The amount of money you earn from your job, your investments, or your business is all a result of your money blueprint. Your subconscious will always validate your blueprint. If you have a blueprint that is set for earning $100,000 per year, that's exactly how well the business will do—enough to earn you about $100,000 per year. The same goes for if you earn $100,000 per year from your job or $100,000 from your investments.

If you are in a job that has the opportunity for bonuses or commission and your blueprint is set for earning $50,000 per year, and you somehow make $80,000 that year, get ready for a terrible year to follow to make up for that extra $30,000 you made the year prior. It has to happen in order to bring you back to the level of your financial blueprint.

On the flipside, if you're set for earning $50,000 and you've been in a slump for a few years, rest assured that you'll get it back. You have to—it's the subconscious law of the mind and money. One way or another, if you're set for $50,000 per year, eventually that's what you will get.

So, back to the original question: How can you tell what your current money blueprint is set for? The most obvious way is to look at your current results.

What is your bank balance?

What is your income?

What is your net worth?

Are you having success with investments?

Are you having success in your business?

Are you a spender or saver?

Do you manage money well?

Are you consistent or inconsistent?

Do you own a business or a job?

Do you stick with one business/job for a long time or do you jump around a lot?

How hard do you work for money?

How are your relationships that involve money?

I once heard a speaker compare your money blueprint to the functionality of a thermostat. If the temperature in the room is 68 degrees, then most likely the thermostat is set for 68 degrees. If someone were to open the window, and its hot outside, the temperature in the room will rise above 68 degrees. What will eventually happen? The thermostat will kick in and bring the temperature back down to 68 degrees. From the example, the only way to permanently change the temperature in the room is to reset the thermostat. In the same way, the only way to change your level of financial success "permanently" is to reset your financial thermostat—your money blueprint.

You can try to get around this all you want. You can develop your knowledge in business and marketing. You can read every book on sales and how to be the shrewdest negotiator. You can become an expert in real estate or the stock market. All of these skills are great "tools," but at the end of the day, without the "inner toolbox" that is big enough and strong enough for you to create and hold on to large amounts of money, all the tools will be useless to you.

Grow Yourself to Grow Your Income!

Regardless if your personal money blueprint is supportive or non-supportive, it will tend to stay with you for the rest life, unless you identify and change it. That is exactly what you will continue to do in this book.

In review, the first element of all change is awareness. Pay attention to yourself and become more self-aware. Observe your thoughts, fears, beliefs, habits, actions, and even inactions. Really put yourself under the microscope, and study yourself to see where some changes may be beneficial to you.

Most of us are under the illusion that we live our lives based on our choices. That's rarely the case. Even for the enlightened amongst us, we might make a few conscious choices throughout the day that reflect our awareness of ourselves, but for the most part, we're robots. We're like robots running on autopilot, ruled by our past programming and old, non-supportive habits.

This is where self-awareness — or should I say our consciousness — comes into play in our lives. Consciousness is observing your thoughts and actions so you can live from true choice in the present moment rather than being controlled by our programming from the past.

By becoming self-aware, we can start to live our lives from who we are today rather than who we were yesterday. This will then allow us to respond appropriately to situations as oppose to reacting inappropriately to events, driven by fears and insecurities of the past. Responding versus reacting is such a powerful way of living our lives. A response will come from your thoughts, whereas a reaction is based in an emotion. Nine times out of 10 that emotion is negative.

Once you become more self-aware, you can see your programming exactly for what it is: information you received and believed in the past, when you were too young to know any better. You can see that your programming is who you learned to be and not necessarily who you are. You can see that you are the "computer" and not the "printer." You are not the "house," but you are the "blueprint." You decide how big or how small the house is. You are not the "app," but the "smartphone." You can erase anything on it that doesn't suit you anymore.

Most of what shapes who you are comes from other people's beliefs and information. Whether this was intentionally done by others or not, this is how we learn as human beings. Sure, there are other aspects that come into play, but for the most part it's our surroundings that mold who we are. Beliefs are not necessarily true or false or right or wrong, but regardless of their validity, beliefs are opinions that are passed around and down from generation to generation, then right on down to you. With this new-found knowledge, you can consciously choose to release any belief that is not supportive to you and your wealth. You can replace those old non-supportive beliefs with new beliefs that propel your life forward.

All of our thoughts are either investments or liabilities. The definition of an investment is "to put to use, by purchase or expenditure, in something offering profitable returns as interest, income, or appreciation in value." In this case, investing the time into becoming more self-aware and conscious of our behaviors will reap exponential returns. A liability, on the other hand, is something disadvantageous. I'm sure you can see how our non-supportive beliefs in regards to money is a liability. Each thought you have will either move you toward success and happiness or further away from it. You will either be empowered or disempowered. That's why it is imperative for you to choose your thoughts and beliefs wisely.

Realize that your thoughts and beliefs are not who you are, and they are not necessarily attached to you. They can be dropped at any time, because they have no more importance than you give them. Nothing has meaning except for the meaning that you give it. If you want instant enlightenment, don't believe a thought you think for now. Gently dismiss the non-supportive thoughts, and slowly start to adopt beliefs that support you—rich beliefs. Remember from earlier, thoughts lead to feelings and feelings lead to actions, which lead to results. You can choose to have a Millionaire Mind Shift and think like wealthy and successful people do, and you'll therefore create the results that wealthy and successful people create. How do successful people think? That's exactly what you will discover in Part Two of this book.

Millionaire Mind Shift

My thoughts are investments, not liabilities.

PART TWO

THE MILLIONAIRE MIND SHIFT

12 Ways the Wealthy Think versus Poor and Middle Class

In Part One of this book, we discussed the mindset for moving forward and manifesting the life that you desire. Everything begins with your thoughts (we discussed how your thoughts lead to feelings, feelings to actions, and actions to results). Don't you think it's amazing that our mind is essentially the basis for our life, but most of us have no clue as to how this thing functions? From a physical standpoint, your mind is nothing more than a really advanced computer system, similar to what you have in your home or office. All of the information you receive is filed away and labeled for easy retrieval later on to help you survive. The key word in the last statement is "survive."

Survive versus Thrive

Anytime you are faced with a situation, you go to the files of your mind to determine how to react. For example, you're presented with a financial opportunity. Without blinking an eye, you automatically go to your folder labeled "Money" and from there decide what to do. The only thoughts you can possibly have about money will be what are stored in your Money folder. That's all you can think about, because that's all that's in that folder.

You make a decision based on what you believe to be logical, sensible, and appropriate for you at the moment. You make, to the best of your knowledge, the right choice. Here's the issue, though: Your "right" choice may not be a successful choice. What makes perfect sense to you, based on your existing Money folder, may be consistently producing poor results. But that's all you know, so what do you do? Repeat the same cycle until now.

For instance, my wife is in a luxury designer store and she sees new shoes that just came out They are just what she had been looking for. She immediately goes to her Money folder in her mind with the question, "Should I get these shoes?" With no delay in response, her mind comes back with the answer, "If they have your size, then it's meant to be. Buy them!" She then happily rushes to the checkout counter, thrilled with the fact that they had her size and the shoes had just come out. I mean, what are the odds?

In her mind, this purchase makes all the sense in the world. She had been looking for a new pair of shoes, she believes she needs them, and they had her size in stock. However, at no point did her mind say, "Sure you've been looking for shoes, and they're right here in front of you, but right now I'm $5,000 in debt from all of the other shoes that I just 'had to have' in the past, so maybe I shouldn't."

Her mind didn't come up with that information because no such file existed in her head. The "When you're in debt, don't buy any more" file was unfortunately never installed in her Money folder, which means that choice wasn't an option. If you've got files in your folder that are non-supportive to your financial success, your choices are limited. These choices will be the natural and automatic decisions that make perfect sense to you. But at the end of the day, they will still produce financial failure or mediocrity.

On the flipside, if you've got files in your Money folder that support financial success, you will automatically and naturally make decisions that produce success. You won't have to think about it. Your natural way of thinking will attract and result in success, kind of like my friend from earlier that goes from one success to another with the Midas Touch. His normal way of thinking produces wealth.

How awesome would it be to naturally think how wealthy and successful people think when it comes to money? I'm imagining you saying, "You bet that would be awesome," or something to that effect. Here's the great news. You can! As stated previously, the first step to change is awareness. Therefore, the first step toward having a Millionaire Mind Shift is to know how wealthy and successful people think.

Wealthy and successful people think very differently from most other people, and that's why the masses are not rich. They think differently from the poor and middle class about money, wealth, themselves, other people, and pretty much every other aspect of life. We're going to examine some of the differences and install new money folders into your mind. With new thoughts and ways of thinking come new choices. You can catch yourself when you are thinking with a poor or middle-class mindset and consciously shift your focus to how wealthy people think. Keep in mind that you have the power to choose to think in ways that support you in your success and happiness in general in life, instead of in ways that don't support you.

First, in no way do I mean to speak down upon or degrade poor people. I have empathy and compassion for their situation. That's part of the reason I wrote this book! I do not believe wealthy people are better than poor people. They're just richer. In an attempt to be sure that you get my message, I'm going to make the distinctions between the rich and the poor as extreme as I possibly can. I won't be referring to the middle-class specifically because that class is endangered, and in the future, there will only be two classes: rich and poor. Also, the middle-class will usually have a mixture of rich and poor mentalities. The goal is for you to become aware of where you fit on the scale and to think more like the wealthy if you want to create financial freedom in your life.

Second, when I discuss the rich and poor, what I am referring to is their mentality — their thought processes and behaviors, rather than the actual amount of money they've got or their value to society. Being broke is temporary, but poor is a mindset.

Third, these will be broad strokes and generalizations to paint the picture of the differences between the rich and the poor. I understand that not all rich and not all poor people are the way I'm describing them to be. Again, my objective is to make sure you get the point of each principle and use them.

Fourth, most of what is being shared in this section may appear to deal more with habits and actions than with ways of thinking. Keep in mind, our actions come from our feelings, which come from our thoughts. Therefore, every rich action is preceded by a rich way of thinking.

Lastly, I'm going to ask that you be willing to let go of being right! Be willing to let go of having to do it your way. Why? Well, your way has gotten you exactly what you've got right now. If you want more of the same, keep doing what you've been doing. If you're not rich already, maybe it's time to consider a different way. It's up to you.

The concepts you are about to learn are profound, yet they seem so simple. They make real changes in people's lives in the real world. How do I know? I've applied these to my life for the past several years and transformed mine. I want to hear from you when you get results as well. If you learn them and use them, I am confident they will transform your life, too.

At the end of each section, you will find actions to take to support you in your Millionaire Mind Shift. It is imperative that you put each Millionaire Mind Shift into action in your life as quickly as possible so the knowledge can create lasting and permanent change.

It's well known that we as humans are creatures of habit. I bet you didn't know that there are actually two kinds of habits: doing habits and not-doing habits. It sounds simple, but everything you are not doing right now, you are in the habit of not doing. The only way to change these not-doing habits into doing habits is to do them. Reading will assist, but it's a whole different ball game when you go from reading to actually doing. If you are truly serious about success, prove it.

Millionaire Mind Shift #1

Play the Game to Win:
Commit to Being Rich

If you want to create wealth, you must play the money game to win and be committed to being rich. If you don't know the rules, then you don't stand a chance at winning. Creating wealth also requires a commitment and intentionality in order to achieve financial success.

All sports or games have rules, and if you were to only have the option to play on defense, what are the chances of winning that game? There is a pretty high likelihood that you will never win by only playing on defense. Poor people play the game of money on defense as oppose to offense. Why is that? Their primary concern is survival instead of creating wealth and abundance in their life. So, now there are a few questions for you: What is your goal? What is your main objective? What is your intention?

Wealthy and successful people's goal is to have massive wealth and abundance—not just enough to get by, but lots and lots of money. What is the goal of most poor people? It's most likely something along the lines of having enough money to pay their bills on time. Is the power of intention evident? When your intention is to have enough to get by, that's exactly what you will get—just enough to get by. The middle class will typically take this one step further and have the elusive intention of being "comfortable." I'm here to break the news to you that being comfortable and being rich are miles apart. Remember earlier, when I said the middle class has a mixture of poor and wealthy ways of thinking? They're aware enough to have the intention to save for a rainy day, but they don't believe they need abundance like the rich. On the other hand, rich people get more wealth and abundance because of what their intentions are.

I've had the pleasure of experiencing all three sides of these views. I've been extremely broke, eating off the fast food value menu once a day. This was when there was $1 cheeseburgers, $1 fries, and $1 desserts. Oh, I'd also have a water to go with that because I couldn't afford to buy a drink. I had a job making $9 per hour, and I was driving my sister's old junk car that she hadn't driven in years. I don't know if you can relate, but this was definitely one of my financial low points.

That lasted for a little less than a year until I got my act together. I then moved up to the level of being comfortable. I have to admit, comfortable feels good when you are coming from eating horrible food once per day. At least now that I was comfortable I could eat more than once per day and sometimes even at a nice restaurant for a change. Even when eating at the nicer restaurants, I made my decisions on what to eat by the numbers next to the meal with the dollar sign. If I saw the forbidden words in the middle-class dictionary, "market price," I'd slowly close the menu and order a drink and an appetizer. I never asked what the market price was, in an attempt to save myself the embarrassment of asking the market price and not ordering.

I must admit, one of the best things about being financially free is not having to pay attention to the price on menus anymore. I make my decisions based on what I have a taste for at the time. I wouldn't dare do that when I was broke or comfortable. Picking up the tab with friends is just an added bonus.

You get what you truly intend to get. If you want to get rich, your goal has to be rich—not just enough to pay bills or be comfortable. Rich means rich! Wealthy people shoot for the moon in everything that they do. Even if they don't hit the moon, they will still be amongst the stars. Poor people don't even shoot for the ceiling in their house and then wonder why they aren't successful. Poor people's goal is to have enough to pay the bills, which is a really low goal.

Wealthy and successful people are committed to being rich. If you were to ask 10 people if they wanted to be rich, they'd light up with a smile and say, "Of course I want to be rich." The unfortunate truth is that most people don't really want to be rich. Why is that? Because they have a lot of negative programming in regards to the accumulation of wealth, which tells them there is something wrong with being rich.

Some possible negative aspects of programming about wealth are:

"What if I become wealthy and lose it all? Then I'll be right back where I am now."

"How will I know if people like me or my money?"

"I'll have to pay Uncle Sam half my money."

"It's too much work to create wealth."

"There's too much responsibility when you're rich."

"Everyone's going to want a handout."

"What if I become a target for kidnapping or robbery?"

"Managing all of that money is a lot of responsibility and requires me to understand investments."

Remember earlier we discussed how each of us has the most powerful computer in the world: our minds, where our Money folder is kept. This folder holds our personal beliefs that include why being rich is important and also why being rich may not. This produces a mixed internal message about wealth. One half of you says, "More money means more freedom and choices in life," but then your other half whispers, "Yeah, but more money means more problems. At least I know how to deal with the problems I have now." One half of you says, "More money would allow me to retire my mom," but then the other side blurts in, "It's going to take a ton of work and working with advisors and stuff. It's so hard to trust people these days." These mixed signals often seem innocent enough and natural, but in reality, they are the major reasons most people never become rich.

Based on the Law of Attraction, you will attract whatever you focus on the most. When you focus on lack and barely getting by, you will get more of that. When you focus on abundance, opportunities will present themselves to you and you will have more than enough. But when your focus is split, the Universe/God/Higher Power doesn't know what you really want. This tripped me up for a while because I viewed this as prudent thinking, as if I'm looking at it from all sides. What's really happening, though, is one minute the universe hears that you want to be rich, so it begins sending opportunities for wealth your way. But then it hears you say, "All rich people are thieves and steal from the poor," so the universe begins to support you in not having much money because you don't want to be a thief.

The main reason most people don't get what they want is that they don't know what they want. Isn't it funny how we always know what we don't want? The next time you hear someone complaining about anything, reply, "So we know what you don't want. What is that you do want from this situation?" You will most likely get an odd look, no response, or both! Wealthy and successful people are totally clear on the fact that they want wealth. The desire and discipline for obtaining wealth and financial freedom is unwavering. They are fully committed to creating wealth. As long as it's moral, ethical, and legal, they will do whatever it takes to have wealth. Rich people do not send mixed messages to the universe with back and forth thinking in regards to wealth.

(When you read that last paragraph, if you felt any negativity toward the sentence, "As long as it's moral, ethical, and legal . . .," you are definitely doing the right thing by reading this book. Can you see how that is such a detrimental way of thinking?)

Poor people have all the good reasons for why being rich might pose a problem. As a result, they are not 100 percent certain they really want to be rich. The message being sent to the universe is confusing. Their messages to people in their lives are confusing. This all happens because their message to themselves is confusing. I know it may be hard to believe, but you always get exactly what you want. But it's important to note that you get what you subconsciously want, not what you say you want. Go ahead and deny this and say, "That's crazy! Who in their right mind would choose to struggle?" In all seriousness, my reply to that is a question: "I don't know. Why would you want to struggle?" Remember earlier, we discussed the power of intention and how you get what you focus on. Your focus is on struggle, so your subconscious mind goes to work to bring you more struggle.

If you are not achieving the wealth you say you desire, there's a good chance that you subconsciously don't really want wealth or you're not willing to do what it takes to actually create that level of wealth. Creating wealth requires intentionality, so you have to really want it. There are three levels of wanting. The first level is, "I want to be wealthy" or "I'll take it if it falls in my lap." This level of wanting is useless. Have you noticed that wanting doesn't necessarily lead to actually having? Also, notice that wanting without actually having leads to more wanting. Wanting becomes habitual and leads to creating a perfect circle that goes nowhere.

Wealth does not come from simply wanting it. How can you verify the validity of this? Simply do a quick internet search for, "What percentage of the population is rich?"

According to the Credit Suisse Global Wealth Report, the world's richest 1 percent — those with more than $1 million — own 44 percent of the world's wealth. Their data also shows that adults with less than $10,000 in wealth make up 56.6 percent of the world's population but hold less than 2 percent of global wealth

. **—inequality.org**

The second level of wanting is, "I'm going to create wealth and financial freedom." This is a conscious decision to become rich. Making the decision to get rich has stronger energy and meshes well with being responsible for creating your own reality. The word decision comes from the Latin word "decidere," which means "to kill off any other alternatives." Making the decision to create wealth is headed in the right direction, but it's not the best.

The third level of wanting is, "I commit to creating wealth and financial freedom." The definition of the word commit is "to pledge (oneself) to a position on an issue or question." This means you're all in and giving 100 percent to achieving wealth. You are willing to do whatever it takes for as long as it takes — no excuses, no maybes, no "I don't feel like it," no ifs, ands, or buts about it. Commitment is: "I will get rich or die trying."

Most people would never truly commit to being rich. If you were to ask them, "Would you bet your life that in the next 10 years you'll be wealthy?" The answer would be no. That's the difference between rich people and poor people. The simple fact that most people won't commit to being rich is the reason they most likely never will be. Some might say, "I work my butt off every day, and I'm trying really hard." but "trying really hard" means nothing.

Another definition for commit is "to bind or obligate," which means you're putting everything you've got into it. You're obligated to this and there are no other options. Most people that I know who are not financially successful put limits on how much they are willing to do, sacrifice, and risk. On the surface, they think they're willing to do whatever it takes, but when questioned deeper, I always find they have conditions around what they are willing to do and not do to succeed.

Here is the not-so-glamorous side of getting rich that I want to get out of the way: Getting rich is not a stroll in the park. Anyone who tells you different is either lacking integrity or knows a lot more than I do and should write a book! I'd sure read it! In my experience, getting rich takes extreme focus, never-give-up attitude, courage, expertise, knowledge, commitment of course, and a wealth mindset. You also have to believe in your heart that you can create wealth and that you absolutely deserve it. At the end of the day, if you are not fully, totally, and truly committed to creating wealth, chances are you won't.

Self-Aware Questions:

Are you willing to work 16-hour days?

Are you willing to work seven days a week?

Are you willing to sacrifice seeing your family and friends?

Are you willing to give up recreations and hobbies?

Are you willing to risk all your time, energy, and start-up capital with no guarantee of returns?

For a short period of time, hopefully, wealthy people are ready and willing to do all of the above. Even if it takes longer than expected, wealth minded people are willing to stay the course until wealth is achieved. Are you? Again, wealthy people are committed enough to do whatever it takes. From my experience, once you fully commit, the universe will bend over backward in support of you.

A few of my favorite quotes on commitment are:

"There's a difference between interest and commitment. When you're interested in doing something, you do it only when circumstances permit. When you're committed to something, you accept no excuses, only results."

— Art Turock

"Stay committed to your decisions, but flexible in your approach."

— Tony Robbins

"You need to make a commitment, and once you make it, then life will give you some answers."

— Les Brown

In other words, the universe will guide you, assist you, support you, and even create miracles for you. All you have to do is fully commit!

Millionaire Mind Shift Action Items

Use a voice recorder and explain why creating wealth is important to you and what your plans are once you create wealth. Be specific. Listen to this at least once per week.

Millionaire Mind Shift #2
Manage Money Well

While most people think that money and the management of money is a financial issue, it is truly a spiritual principle. The subject of money, finances, and wealth is mentioned in the Bible more than 800 times. It's safe to say that this is pretty important to God, and He knew we would always have to deal with this no matter the form our money takes. In the Bible, your wealth was measured by your land, livestock, and possessions. Today, wealth is measured in assets that are purchased with money.

Depending on your background, you may or may not be familiar with the word "tithing." Tithing is giving the first 10 percent of your income to God through your local church. I'm sure you're wondering, "Why is he discussing tithing in a chapter about managing money well?" Believers and non-believers have argued for centuries about the subject of tithing in regards to managing your finances. Some religions refer to tithing as the "single best investment" anyone can make. While I do believe this is true, I want to use the term "investment" loosely here because I don't want you to think of tithing as you would think of an investment in the stock market. We are instructed to tithe as a Biblical principle as the basis for managing our finances. The tithe to your church is the fuel that empowers the church to reach more people, grow, and pay the bills. The subject of tithing can be a bit touchy for some because of bad past experiences. You may have tithed to a church you felt was not doing the right things with the tithes, for example. I recommend tithing to a church that you feel is active in the community, growing its congregation, and Biblically based in their teachings. Or, maybe you're currently struggling with your finances and you're thinking there is no way you can survive without that 10 percent of your income when you are already living paycheck to paycheck. I completely understand this, too, because I have been on both sides of this equation. Tithing is the basis for getting your finances in order. What you've done up until this point has gotten you to where you are. If you are not where you would like to be financially, then I recommend trying God's way to approach your finances.

I was raised in a Baptist Christian household, so tithing was never an option for me growing up. I remember my dad giving me and my siblings $1 each, then turning around and giving us change for the dollar so we could give our 10-cent tithe in church.

Tithing is a Biblical principle that I adhere to in managing my finances. In my opinion, the first step to managing your money well is to adopt the habit of tithing. Tithing is a step of faith, placing your trust in God that all of our needs will be taken care of with 10 percent less of our income. This, taken at face value, defies human logic. I can hear someone saying to me now, "So you mean to tell me that I can do more with 90 percent of my income as opposed to 100 percent?" Think of it this way: If it weren't for the functions of our bodies and abilities that have been given to us by God, we would not be able to go make a living. God only requires us to give 10 percent back to Him in order to grow the local church. The 90 percent that's leftover is yours to do whatever you choose. That's a pretty sweet deal if you think about it. God will bless you to make enough to live in abundance, and all he asks is that you tithe 10 percent of your income. Then, the remaining 90 percent will be blessed. Keep only 90 percent and God will reap far better rewards for you than for you to continue mismanaging 100 percent of your finances.

Now I know for some this is a difficult concept to grasp, but I encourage you to try it for 12 months. This is the only subject in the

Bible that God asks you to test Him on. Tithing has made my life what it is today — faith that God and my 90 percent far exceed what I can do with 100 percent of my income. Tithing will increase your faith and cause money miracles in your life. Gaining freedom in your life and gaining control of your finances starts with believing that God has a good plan for your life, including your finances.

The second step after laying a solid foundation with tithing is to manage what's left. There is a best-selling book, The Millionaire Next Door, that surveyed a group of millionaires and asked how they attained their wealth. What do you think the #1 common thread amongst them would be? Despite what we see on "The Lifestyles of the Rich and Famous," most would think all wealthy people have really expensive taste and throw money around like it grows on trees. The truth is that wealthy people are good at managing their money. Sure, there are some exceptions to this rule, but for the most part, wealthy and successful people manage their money well. Poor people mismanage their money. I can hear you saying now, "Sure it's easy to manage money when you have a bunch of it lying around."

Wealthy people are not any smarter than poor people, though. The difference is that wealthy people have more supportive money habits. As discussed earlier, these money habits are mostly built on our past programming. So, if you're not managing your money well, you were probably programmed not to manage your money well. Then there is also the chance that you simply don't know how to manage your money in an effective way that works for you. Unfortunately for me, I grew up in a low-income neighborhood and I don't remember Money Management 101 being offered. Money Management 101 wasn't even offered at the college I attended. Instead we learned about the Pythagorean Theorem, which is obviously something I use on a daily basis . . . not.

I know this isn't a glamorous, mind-blowing topic, but it comes down to this very basic principle: One of the biggest differences between financial success and financial failure is whether you manage money well or not. In order to master money, you must manage money. Poor people mismanage their money or completely avoid the subject of money altogether. Many people don't like to manage their money because they work hard for it and they don't want to feel restricted. Then of course, as I mentioned earlier, they say they don't have enough money to manage.

As far as the first excuse, managing your money does the complete opposite of restrict you. Managing your money actually promotes your freedom. Managing your money well, over a period of time, allows you to eventually create financial freedom so working is an option. In my opinion, that's real freedom.

As for those using the, "I don't have enough money to manage" rationale, you're viewing this a little backwards. The reality is that when you begin to manage your money, you will have more money to manage, as opposed to the story you've been telling yourself of, "When I have plenty, I'll begin to manage it." That's "putting the cart before the horse," as my granddad used to say. Saying, "I'll start managing my money well when I have plenty" is like a person wanting to lose weight saying, "I'll start working out as soon as I lose this weight." Once you start to manage the money you currently have, no matter the amount, you will inevitably have more money to handle. The universe we live in is kind and loving, and the rule is if you want more, you've got to show that you can handle what you've already got.

I'm reminded of a situation that I had in my earlier days of fixing and flipping houses, as an example. I started out with a contractor who was extremely knowledgeable and did really good work. He would never tell me no to any of my requests, and he would promise me the moon would be torn down and rebuilt by the end of the week. But as great as his work and promises were, he would never complete a project on time. Of course, we all know time is money, so this wasn't going to work long-term. We would have conversations with the contractor about this issue, but nothing really changed. As time progressed and the business grew with more projects going on simultaneously, the projects continued to fall behind schedule.

My business partner had secured additional funding, which would allow us to triple our capacity for properties. We scheduled a meeting with our contractor to discuss bringing on some additional contractors to help him, and that we wanted him to work with the other contractors because he understood our process. The contractor insisted on being able to take on the additional workload as well—without the additional help.

Now here's the question. Being the savvy business person, yet a decent person in general, would you allow the contractor to bid the additional work? Your initial response might be, "Sure," because he does really good work, is dependable, and has been with you since inception. But when considering a little more deeply, the response may be, "No," because why would you want to set the contractor up to fail? The contractor couldn't even handle one to two projects at a time, so how could he possibly handle three times the work? The same thing holds true when it comes to the universe and you. You have to show you can handle what you've got first.

You must acquire the habits and skills of managing a small amount of money before you can manage a large amount of money. Always keep in mind that we are creatures of habit. Creating the habit of managing your money is more important than the amount. So how do you manage your money? There are many different gurus and effective money management methods that are beyond the scope of this book to go over every detail. My recommendation is to explore some and see what feels the best for you. Managing your money well is meant to empower you and thrust you toward financial freedom. So, if the first money management system doesn't resonate with you, keep searching until you find one that fits. This isn't a one-size-fits-all type of deal. Find a system that works for you, but learn to manage your money regardless.

Let me give you a couple of the basics to get you started. Open a separate bank account designated for future investments. Put 10 percent of every dollar you receive into this bank account (after taxes, of course). The money in this account is only to be used for investments that create passive income. This separate bank account's only job is to buy your financial freedom. You will buy your financial freedom one investment at a time until your passive income exceeds your earned income. At that point, you will have achieved financial freedom. Working daily, at that point, has become an option for you. You get to spend the income from the passive investments, but never the principal itself. In this way, it always keeps growing and you can never go broke.

It doesn't matter if you are starting with only a dollar to allocate to this account. The magic is in creating the habit of saving for investments. I know you may be thinking, "How am I supposed to get financially free from saving $1 per pay period?" You just have to get started and commit to doubling that dollar every month.

It would look something like this:

Month 1: $2

Month 2: $4

Month 3: $8

Month 4: $16, $32, $64, etc.

By the 12th month, you could be up to saving $2,048 per month, with a total savings account of more than $4,000! This is with you starting with only saving $1 per pay period. I use $1 as an example because everyone can get started, even if it is only a dollar. Hopefully you are starting with more, but you can get started even if you only have $1 to begin with. When you learn some of the strategies that I teach on how to supercharge this savings account, you can reap some amazing fruits from your efforts in a relatively short amount of time. Within two years, you could easily be putting $10,000 per month directly into your financial freedom account! Imagine developing the habit of managing money so well that when a bonus check arrives at work, you don't need the money for anything. So, you deposit the entire bonus into your account for buying your freedom. I've got one even better for you — imagine forgetting when your payday is!

It doesn't matter if you have a fortune already or virtually nothing. What matters most is that you immediately begin to manage what you've got, and you will be amazed at how soon you get more. There is a bit more than just a physical principle in play here; there is a spiritual principle at play here as well. Money miracles will occur once you demonstrate to the universe that you can handle your finances properly.

In addition to opening a separate account designated for investments, find a place to deposit your spare change each day. If you want to take it a step further like me, step it up to $1 bills and $5 bills, too. The amount getting started doesn't matter, because you can always work your way up. What's important is for you to create the habit by placing daily attention on your objective, which is becoming financially free. Just as like attracts like, money attracts more money. These habits will attract more and more money opportunities for financial freedom into your life.

Although I think saving 10 percent of your income for long-term investing is extremely powerful, I really enjoy having an equal opposite account. The opposite account is designed specifically for you to "blow" the money and have some fun. One of the biggest, unknown, secrets to managing money is balance. You're torn between wanting to save as much money as possible for investment and growth while also contributing another 10 percent of your income into a "play account." Actually, my "play account" is my pocket. You should withdraw 10 percent of your income in cash. Why? Because we are human beings and holistic in nature. You cannot affect one part of your life without affecting the others. Some people will save, save, save until that rainy day comes along and wipes that savings out. Here goes your fun side, saying, "I knew we should've spent that money on something fun." But then your logical self is fulfilled, saying, "Well if we didn't save, we wouldn't have had the money for the rainy day." That's your old way of thinking. Set yourself up for success by saving to invest and setting aside 10 percent of your income to have fun.

On the other hand, if all you do is spend, not only will you never become rich, but the responsible, more logical part of you will also eventually create a situation in which you don't even enjoy the things you spend your money on. You will develop an uneasy feeling of guilt. That guilt will then cause you to unconsciously overspend as a way of expressing your emotions. Although you may feel better temporarily, the guilt of not managing your money well will return. This is a vicious cycle, and the only way to break out is to learn how to manage your money in a way that works.

Your "fun money" is used to do the things you wouldn't normally do. This does not include your necessities. This is for the extra-special things like flying first-class on your family vacation, renting a limo for a special night on the town with a loved one, or floor seats at your favorite team's ball game. Maybe your fun money is used for something as simple as a full-body massage and facial to make you feel like a king. It's up to you, as long as whatever it is makes you feel rich while doing it. Ideally, you want to spend all your fun money each month. Eventually when your income is supercharged, you can save your "fun money" for a few months and buy a big-ticket item. For example, I collect luxury watches, so I may put off spending my "fun money" for a month or two to buy a Rolex. I make a game out of it nowadays, and I can't wait to blow my "fun money." You'll feel the same, too!

The only way that most of us will ever continue to follow our saving plan is by offsetting it with a "plan to play" that rewards you along the way for your efforts. Your "fun money" account has a dual purpose. It also strengthens your "receiving" muscle in regards to money. Having a "fun account" makes managing money a whole lot more fun, too. In addition to tithing, saving for investments, and the fun account, I advise that you create three more accounts:

- Long-term savings: 10 percent
- Continuing education: 10 percent
- Necessities: 50 percent

Most poor people think that it's all about how much money you make. They believe you have to earn a fortune to get rich. This is where they beat themselves before they even start. The fact is that if you manage your money as described above, you can become financially free on a relatively small income. Even if you have a huge yearly income, if you mismanage your money, you can't become financially free. This is why you see so many high-income professional athletes, attorneys, doctors, and actors who are basically broke. This is because what you are doing with the money coming in is more important than the amount that's coming in.

This is not a habit that comes natural to most. In the beginning, it may feel like a lot of work, and you may wonder if it's actually worth it. If you've ever tried to get into any kind of physical shape, you can compare managing your finances to preparing for a triathlon. In the beginning of training, you will be stiff and sore after each training session. You will dread the running and how your lungs will burn from all of the cardio training, but you keep going because you know that in order to become a top triathlete, you have to push through and accept the temporary pain as part of what it took to succeed. After a few months, you will begin to actually enjoy running and training and start to actually look forward to training each day.

This is exactly what will happen to you in the arena of money management. Just like training for a triathlon, you start out hating every moment, but eventually you'll be excited to get your paycheck and divide it into the different accounts! You may even have to control yourself and keep from bringing this up to your friends every chance you get. (Don't tell other people what you're doing, because they won't care.) If you want to share these concepts with someone, buy them a copy of this book instead.

At the end of the day, it all boils down to this: Either you manage your money, or it will manage you. Money is such a big part of life, when you learn how to get your finances under control, all other areas of your life will soar.

Millionaire Mind Shift Action Items

Start managing your money today, from wherever you are.

Open a savings account for investments only, 10 percent

Designate a place in your home to collect loose change.

Withdraw 10 percent of income as "fun money."

Create three accounts:

- Long-term savings: 10 percent
- Continuing education: 10 percent
- Necessities: 50 percent

Millionaire Mind Shift #3
Focus on Building Net Worth

When it comes to money, most people in our society speak in terms of, "How much do you make?" Very seldom do you hear, "What's your net worth?" Few people talk in this way, except the wealthy 5 percent of our population and Forbes, of course. In Forbes, the financial discussion is almost always centered around net worth of celebrities and pro athletes, like, "Warren Buffet sold X number of shares in ABC company, and that increased his net worth by $2 billion," or "The stock market drop last quarter caused billionaires to lose $1 trillion in combined net worth."

The true measure of wealth is net worth, not working income. This is a never-changing fact. Net worth is the financial value of everything you own. In order to determine what your net worth is, add up the value of everything you own, and subtract everything that you owe. This includes your cash, investment accounts, real estate, current value of your business if you own one, value of your residence if you own one, and any jewelry or art you own. Then subtract all your debt from the total. Net worth is the ultimate measure of wealth because, if necessary, what you own can be liquidated into cash.

Wealthy people understand the difference between working income and net worth. There is a huge distinction between the two. Working income is a piece of the puzzle that determines your net worth. The four pillars of net worth are:

1. Income
2. Savings
3. Investments
4. Simplification

In order to build a high net worth, rich people understand that the wealth equation requires all four pillars. Each pillar is essential and important, so they must all be there in order to create high, indestructible net worth that will last for generations to come. Let's examine each one.

Beginning with number one, which is income, it has two forms: working income and passive income. Working income is earned by actively doing something in exchange for income, such as a paycheck from your job. This also includes the profits or income taken from a business if you are an entrepreneur. Working income is basically you trading your time for dollars, whether that is hourly, salaried, or profits from your business. Working income is essential because, without it, it's pretty much impossible to address the other three pillars of net worth. Our working income is how we fill up our financial "pipeline," in a sense. The more income you earn, the more you can save and invest. Again, although working capital is critical, it is only valuable as a part of the entire net worth equation. Most poor and many middle-class people only focus on working income, unfortunately. As a result, they end up with a low net worth or none at all.

The second form of income is my favorite, which is passive income. Passive income is money earned without you actively working. We will discuss passive income in more depth later, but for now, think of it as another source of income filling the pipeline, which can be used for spending, saving, and investing.

Having a savings is essential to creating a high net worth. You can earn all of the money in the world, but if you can't hang on to any of it, you will never create wealth. Most people are wired with a financial blueprint to spend. Whatever money they have is spent. We are surrounded by ads and marketing plans that are designed to encourage us to spend money all of the time. We're encouraged to choose immediate gratification over long-term balance. These spenders can be identified by mottos like, "It's just money," which is why they don't have much of it, or they say something like, "it's my money so I spend it how I like." They usually have a credit card bill that's larger than their income for an entire year. Another thing people often say is, "I don't have the money right now." The first step is to create income to fill the pipeline, and then the savings is to keep it there. Without these two pillars, it is impossible to address the next pillar for building your net worth.

Once you've created the habit of saving money and you've begun saving a decent portion of your income, then you can move to the next pillar and make your money multiply through investing. Investing is a game that is well worth learning to play. Generally speaking, the better you are at investing, the faster your money can grow and create an even greater net worth. Wealthy people take the time to learn about investing and all of the different investment classes. They spend their energy deciding what investment vehicles fit their goals. They pride themselves on gaining knowledge on to be excellent investors or at least hire excellent investors to do it for them. Wealthy people will research and hire experts to consult with or invest for them. Poor people think investing is only for rich people, so they never take the time to learn about it and they stay broke.

The fourth and final pillar of building a high net worth is recognized by very few people as important in creating wealth, which is something called simplification. Simplification is where you consciously create a lifestyle where you need less money to live on. By decreasing your cost of living, you increase your savings and the amount of funds available for investing. Ideally, you want to start with saving 10 percent of your income, but as you implement all of the strategies in this book and the strategies I teach, hopefully you will increase that to 20 percent. Eventually your income can increase so much that you can flip the equation on its head, where you only need 10 percent of your income to live on, and you invest the other 70 percent! What kind of life would that be for you? How much good could you do with that kind of freedom? The possibilities are limitless.

To illustrate the power of simplification, here's a story about Joe. When Joe was only 20 years old, he made a wise choice and purchased a home. He paid $120,000 for a foreclosure. Eight years later when the housing market recovered, Joe sold his home for $210,000, meaning he profited just under $100,000. Joe considered buying a new home with the proceeds, but decided to invest the money with his brother who flips houses for a 10 percent return on his money every 90 days. He also began buying rental properties for passive income. Joe decided to simplify his lifestyle for a few years and live in a studio apartment downtown in order to focus on investing. Now at the age of 32, Joe is financially free. Joe won his financial freedom not through earning a ton of money, but by consciously scaling back his personal overhead. Yes, he still works, because he enjoys what he does for a living, but working is now an option. In fact, he only works eight months out of the year. He takes month-long vacations each quarter. How many people do you know who would love to spend four months of the year traveling on vacation, never really having to work again? At the ripe old age of 32? It's all because Joe created a simple lifestyle and made wise investments. Now he lives his life on his own terms.

So, what will it take for you to be happy financially? It's totally up to you. You can set the bar as high as living in a 10,000 square-foot mansion with three vacation homes, and 10 exotic cars, eating caviar and drinking the world's best champagne if you want. Or, maybe you don't need all of the toys to be happy, and you just want to have work as an option for you and your family. Whichever you choose will determine how long it will take you to hit that goal. Either goal, as described above or somewhere in between, is fine, as long as your new goal is your personal goal and nobody else's.

Building your net worth is a four-pillar equation. As an analogy, imagine trying to drive a car with only one wheel. What would that ride be like? You'd probably struggle and go in circles, if the car will even go anywhere at all. Sound familiar? Poor and middle-class people play the money game on one wheel. They are usually under the belief that the only way to get rich is to earn a lot of money. Their belief is that way because they've never been in that position, so their perspective is limited. Unfortunately, most don't understand Parkinson's Law: "Expenses will always rise in direct proportion to income." Alternatively, wealthy people play the game of money on all four wheels. That's why their ride is relatively easy and smooth.

We've all witnessed this either in our own lives or someone else's: You have a perfectly fine, working car that's paid for. Once you make more money, you get a better car. You have a house. Once you make more money, you buy a bigger house. You have nice clothes. Once you make more money, you get nicer clothes. Of course, there are exceptions to this rule, but not many! In general, when income increases, expenses almost invariably go up as well. This is why income alone will never create wealth.

This book is called the Millionaire Mind Shift. Why didn't I name it Million Bucks per Year Income to Be Rich? Well, you don't need to make $1 million per year to be a millionaire. The term "millionaire" refers to net worth, not income. If your intention is to be a millionaire or more, you must focus on building your net worth, which is based on more than just your income.

Make it a habit to track your net worth at least quarterly. By tracking your net worth, you are focusing on it. What you focus on will expand. This holds true for all other areas of your life as well. What you track increases. I encourage you to start researching and increasing your financial literacy. Take the time to learn about the different investment vehicles available to you on a surface level. You should only gain a basic knowledge about an investment vehicle, then seek a professional in that area. Otherwise you may fall into "analysis paralysis" which means that you may end up "researching" for the next few years and never make a move. Creating wealth requires intentionality and the ability to take action when needed. When you take the time to learn before taking any action, you will set yourself up for success.

There's a quote I like that holds true in this situation: "The only shortcuts in life are mentors." A mentor can come in many forms, so always be open and willing to learn from people who have already been where you're headed. Mentors can be one-on-one non-paid mentorships, one-on-one paid mentorships, consultants, financial planners, financial advisors, books, courses, and many other sources. These professionals can help you track and build your net worth.

The best way to find a good professional in anything is to seek a referral from a friend or associate who is happy with the person they're using. I'm not saying you should take everything that these professionals say as gospel. I personally differ from many financial planners as far as my investment strategies. What you decide to do is solely up to you, but it always helps to hear a professional's perspective. What I am suggesting is that you find a qualified professional with the skills in a particular area to help you plan and track your finances. A good professional will provide you with knowledge and recommendations to help you build the investing habits that will produce wealth. Generally, I recommend finding professionals in specific areas as opposed to the planners who work with an array of financial products. In that way, you maintain a level of control and balance by hearing unrelated perspectives on your investment strategies. Then you can make an informed decision on what's right for you.

Millionaire Mind Shift Action Items

Focus on all four pillars of net worth:

- Income
- Savings
- Investments
- Simplification

Calculate your net worth: (Your Assets) – (Your Liabilities) = Net Worth

Track your net worth each quarter.

Start researching the many different types of investing you think will interest you via web searches, videos, and social media.

Ask friends who invest for referrals.

Millionaire Mind Shift #4
Make Money Work for You

Most people grew up being programmed with the idea that you have to work hard for money. If a man doesn't work, then he doesn't deserve to eat. This led us to believe that if we wanted more money, then we'd better start working harder. Alongside this idea, though, is the idea that it's just as important to make your money work hard for you. I'd bet there is a good chance you were never taught that!

It's not my intention to take away from the fact that working hard is important. Working hard is important, but working hard alone will never make you wealthy. How do we know? Just take a look around you right now in your world. There are millions of people in your city, and billions of people in the world, who slave away at their jobs every day and sometimes night, too. Are they all wealthy? Nope! Are the majority of them wealthy? Nope! Are there a lot of them that are wealthy? Unfortunately, most of them are broke or pretty close to it. On the other hand, who do you see frolicking around at a coffee shop in the afternoon with a double pump latte? Who spends their afternoons playing golf, tennis, racquet ball, or sailing? Who spends more time on vacation than they do in their second home? Who spends their days shopping with friends to pass time before happy hour? Who gets a call from their accountant telling them they need to spend X amount of dollars before the year ends or you'll get creamed in taxes? Rich people, that's who! So, let's dispel the faulty idea that you have to work hard to get rich!

There is nothing wrong with hard work, as long as you know what to do with your "hard work's" pay. Knowing what to do with that money is where you move from hard work to smart work. Use your hard work as a benchmark for how hard your money should work for you. Wealthy people can spend their days seeming to be relaxed because they work smart. They employ other people and their own money to work for them. Working hard for their money is something that wealthy people understand is only temporary. Wealth minded people understand that you have to work hard until your money works hard enough to take your place. They understand that the more their money works, the less they will have to work. At that point, you are financially free and continuing to work becomes an option.

Think of money as energy. Generally speaking, most people put work energy in and get money energy out. The people who achieve financial freedom have learned how to substitute their investment of work energy with other forms of energy. Examples of these other forms of energy include other people's work, business systems/technology, or investment capital at work. To recap, the name of the game is, "First you work hard for money, then you let money work hard for you."

It's hard to win at the money game if you don't have a goal. Most people don't have a clue what it takes to win. What's your goal? How do you know when you have won? How do you know when the game is over? Are you shooting for $100,000 a year in income, $100,000 a month in income, becoming a millionaire, becoming a multimillionaire? My goal is for you to not have to work unless you choose to do so by choice instead of necessity. The goal is to become financially free as quickly as possible. My definition of financial freedom is the ability to live the lifestyle you desire from the income of your own personal resources. Notice how my definition of financial freedom isn't a particular dollar amount. Only you can decide what your desired lifestyle is.

Because there is a good chance that your desired lifestyle is going to cost money, you will need to earn money without working to be "free." As discussed in the previous chapter, we refer to income without work as passive income. In order to win the money game, the goal is for your passive income to pay for your desired lifestyle. Financial freedom occurs when your passive income exceeds your expenses.

There are two primary sources of passive income. The first is "business working for you." This is generating ongoing income from businesses you do not need to be personally involved with in order for that business to operate and yield an income. Examples include rental real estate, owning storage units, vending machines, or ATMs, royalties from music, books, or software, licensing your ideas, patents on inventions, network marketing, and becoming a franchisor, just to name a few. This form of passive income also includes setting up any business under the sun or moon that is systematized to work without you. Now, reread that last sentence again. To qualify as a passive income, it has to be systematized and work without you. The idea is that the business is working and producing value for people — instead of you doing the work.

Network marketing is an amazing concept because it usually doesn't require you to put up a lot of upfront capital. Secondly, once you've done the initial work, it allows you to enjoy ongoing residual income for years to come. Residual income is very close to passive income and is very powerful as well. It is yet another form of income without you working. Network marketing is something you can start on the side in addition to your main source of income. The same holds true for buying and holding real estate for rentals and affiliate marketing online. All of this can be done on your time from 7 to 12 p.m. after your 9 to 5 day job.

The second major source of passive income is money working for you. This includes investment earnings from financial instruments, like, stocks, bonds, treasury bills, money markets, or mutual funds. A different kind of example would be owning mortgages or any other asset that appreciates in value and can be liquidated for cash.

I can't overemphasize the importance of creating passive income as quickly as possible. Without passive income, you can never be free. It's that simple. Although the term "passive income" may not be new to you, did you know that most people have a tough time creating passive income? There are three main reasons as to why, and you guessed the first one, I'm sure: conditioning. Most of us were conditioned to not earn passive income. I, for one, had never even heard of passive income until I was an adult. Think back to when you became around driving age and you needed money to buy a car. What did your parents tell you? Did they say, "If you want a car, you'd better go earn some passive income to pay for it"? Of course not! Most of us heard, "Get a job," Save your money," or something to that effect. Our parents taught us what was passed down from their parents — to "work" for money. Our upbringing is what makes passive income abnormal for most of us.

The second reason most people have a tough time earning passive income is because most haven't taken the time to learn about it on their own. Again, I don't remember Passive Income 101 being offered at any school from K–12, and I don't remember it being offered at the college I attended either. Because we didn't learn about creating passive income in school, we must've learned it at home, right? Doubt it. So, most of us don't know much about it, or that it even exists, and therefore don't do much about it.

Lastly, because we were never exposed to passive income and investing, we have never given it the correct amount of attention. We have lived our lives, for the most part, and based our career choices on generating working income. How different would your career choices have been if you understood from an early age that a primary financial goal was to create passive income?

You will have the best of both worlds when you make the decision to choose business opportunities that immediately or eventually produce passive income—working income now and passive income later. I encounter quite a few people who either work a job or own service businesses in which they have to be there personally to make money. There's nothing wrong with being in a personal service business, except that unless you start investing soon and do exceptionally well, you will be trapped into working forever. Refer back a few paragraphs to review some of the passive business income options discussed.

The fact of the matter is this: Almost everyone has a money blueprint that is set for earning working income and against earning passive income. This attitude can be changed by what we discussed earlier in the book. Thoughts lead to actions and actions lead to results. Change your money blueprint so earning a massive passive income is normal and natural for you.

Wealthy and successful people think in terms of the long game. They are more focused on investing for freedom tomorrow while balancing their spending for enjoyment today. Poor people think short term. They want instant gratification. Their excuse for this sounds like, "How can I think about tomorrow when I have to worry about surviving today?" This creates a vicious cycle, because eventually tomorrow will become today; so, if you haven't taken care of today's problem, you'll be saying the same thing tomorrow, too.

If you want to increase your wealth, you either have to earn more or live on less. You have the power to make the choice of what house you live in, the kind of car you drive, the clothes you wear, or the food you have to eat. Nobody has a gun to your head; it's a simple matter of priorities. Wealthy people choose balance, while poor people choose now.

I think about my parents. For 23 years, my dad worked for the US Postal Service, and my mom was a stay-at-home mom. My parents' income came from my dad working and, whenever he could, working overtime. They saved what was left over after taking care of a family of seven. We ate out once per month on Sunday after church, they didn't buy fancy clothes, and they didn't drive the latest car. We lived comfortably, but modestly, and they eventually paid off their mortgage and their cars. At the age of 61, by saving and investing into a pension plan, my dad was able to retire. My parents had a middle-class mindset, and it happened to work out for him to retire with a pension plan, but those rearely exist anymore.

Buying things for instant gratification is nothing more than an attempt to make up for your dissatisfaction in life. More often than not, spending money you don't have comes from expending emotions that you do have. This is commonly known as "retail therapy." The act of needing immediate gratification actually has very little to do with the actual item you're buying and more so to do with a lack of fulfillment in your life. If overspending isn't coming from your emotions, then it is coming from your money blueprint. Regardless of how the issue has come up, it must be dealt with accordingly.

Let's take a look at Char's story. Char was one of my mentees, and in her eyes, her parents were the textbook example of cheapskates. They used coupons for everything. Her mother would take her and her siblings grocery shopping and have the kids make purchases because the store had a limit on how many items one could purchase with coupons. Her father drove a 30-plus-year-old car that often broke down while taking her to and from school. Her family never flew when they took a vacation, but drove for days across country to save money. Her parents even made them reuse paper towels!

Everything was "too expensive." The way Char's parents acted, she thought her parents were broke. But her parents earned a decent income, so she believed, at around $60,000 a year at the time. She was totally confused. Char despised her parents' stingy habits so much that she became the complete opposite. As an adult, she didn't want anything to do with it unless it was high-class and expensive. She moved out on her own, and didn't realize it, but in a flash, she had spent all the money she makes each week and then some! Char had all of the credit cards she could apply for, membership cards, and anything else you can think of. The balances were all maxed out and she couldn't even make the minimum payments when I met her. After implementing the principles in this book, Char's life was never the same. Her whole world changed. She came to realize that her behavior was a form of resentment toward her parents for being so cheap. It was also to prove to herself that she was nothing like them. Char now says she no longer has the urge to spend her money in "stupid" ways.

Now when Char is walking in the mall and sees an item she would bought in the past, she searches her more supportive, wealth-building files. Her more supportive file says, "You'd be much better off putting that money into your savings for your financial freedom instead." Char would then put the item on hold until the next day instead of buying it right there in the moment as usual. She usually never went back to get the item.

Char had successfully replaced her "instant gratification" files with "financial freedom" files. She wasn't programmed to spend anymore. She now knows that it is fine to hang on to what her parents modeled, as far as saving money, but at the same time, to treat herself to nice things with her "fun money." Char also sent both of her parents a copy of this book so they could be more balanced, too. Char understands she doesn't have to be as "cheap" as her parents were to be a millionaire, but she also has the clarity now to see that if she spends her money unconsciously as she did before, she will never achieve financial freedom.

Again, the idea is to have your money work as hard for you as you do for it. That means you have to save and invest as opposed to making it your life's mission to spend it all. It's almost funny how rich people have a lot of money and spend a little, while on the flipside, poor people have a little money and spend a lot. Wealthy people work to earn money to pay for their investments: long-term focus. Poor people work to earn money to live today: short-term focus. These are two totally different ways to look at life. Wealthy people buy assets, things that will likely go up in value. Poor people buy expenses, things that will go down in value. Wealthy people collect passive income checks. Poor people collect bills.

My biased recommendation for investments is to buy real estate. Ninety percent of the world's millionaires became so through real estate. For the average investor, real estate offers the best way to develop significant wealth. It's best if you can purchase property that can produce positive cash flow, but at the end of the day, any real estate is better than no real estate. Just like any other investment, real estate has its ups and downs, but in the end, you can bet it will be worth more than it is today. Whether it be five, 10, 20, or 30 years from now, it could be all you need to get rich.

Buy what you can afford as soon as possible. If you need more capital to get started, you can partner with people you trust and know. The only way I see for you to get into trouble with real estate is to overleverage yourself or to sell in a down market. At the time of writing this, real estate has just recently hit its peak in the US. There is always massive opportunity in a down market. Over the next couple of years, there will be a huge wealth transfer. Hopefully you will be one of the few to whom wealth will be shifting. If you implement my earlier advice and manage your money properly, the likelihood of a real estate deal going bad will be slim to none. I'm sure you've heard the saying, "Don't wait to buy real estate; buy real estate and wait."

While poor people often have the view of a dollar earned today being a dollar to trade for something they want right now, wealthy people see every dollar as a little soldier that can go to work on their behalf, for their financial freedom. Those soldiers will bring back hundreds more, which can then be redeployed to earn a thousand more dollars. Think about it like this: Every dollar you spend today may actually cost you a hundred dollars tomorrow. Every single dollar I receive is an "investment soldier," and that soldier's sole mission is my financial freedom. I'm really careful with my "freedom fighters" to not to get rid of them quickly or easily.

The key to making this all work together is to get educated. As stated earlier, wealthy and successful people take the time and energy to learn about the investment world. Become familiar with a variety of different investment vehicles and financial instruments, such as real estate, stocks, bonds, funds, trade accounts, currency exchange — the full spectrum. Pick one to get started in and become an expert. Begin investing in that area, then diversify your profits into more later.

In review, poor people work hard and spend all their money, which results in their having to work hard forever. Wealthy people work hard, save, and then invest their money so that working hard, or working at all for that matter, is an option.

Millionaire Mind Shift Action Items

Get educated:

- Search the internet for more information about investment groups.
- Read at least one investment book per month.
- Read magazines: Money, Forbes, etc.
- Choose an area to become an expert in and begin investing.

Focus on three ways to create income outside of your current main source of income. Begin researching, then take action on these strategies.

Buy real estate and wait.

Millionaire Mind Shift #5
Open and Willing to Receive

The average person does not reach their full potential for many reasons, but there is one that really stands out: most people are poor "receivers." What you will find is that whether they are good at giving or not, most people are bad at receiving. Because of this, they don't receive much. In general, people are challenged with receiving for several reasons.

The first major reason most people have a problem with receiving is because of the saying, "It's better to give than receive." That is a loaded statement that is, in most cases, propagated by people and groups who want you to give and themselves to receive. This statement puts all of the emphasis on the "giving" portion of the equation, but what about the receiving part? Giving and receiving go hand in hand. You can't have one without the other. For every giver, there must be a receiver, and vice versa.

Think about this for a moment. How could you give if there wasn't someone or something there to receive? Both have to work together in perfect balance. So, if giving and receiving must always balance each other out, then it's safe to say giving and receiving are equally important. I mean, how good does it feel to give? If you're like me, you'd agree that giving is one of the most wonderful and fulfilling things to do. Conversely, think of how it feels when you want to give and the other person isn't willing to receive. Of course, it feels terrible. In the future, if you are not willing to receive, then you are "cheating" those that want to give to you. If you aren't willing to receive, it will go to someone who is open and willing to receive. That's one of the reasons the rich get richer and the poor get poorer—not because of greed, but because they are willing to receive, so they receive a lot.

I learned this lesson in a weird way. If you were to place a bucket outside in a rainstorm overnight, by morning the bucket will be full of rainwater. All of the ground under and around the bucket is dry, but the bucket has rainwater. This is an example of how abundant nature is. If one part is dry, another part is doubly wet. The rain water accumulated in the bucket because it was open and willing to receive. This is similar to how money works. There is plenty of money floating all around us in abundance, and it has to go somewhere. Here's the secret: If people aren't willing to receive their share, the money will go to whoever will receive. The rain doesn't care who the recipient is, and money doesn't either.

It feels amazing and natural to be open and willing to receive. Anything you've made up to contradict this is just a "story" that isn't serving you or anyone else, for that matter. Let your money come in by letting your story go.

The second major reason most people have a problem with receiving is a feeling of being unworthy or undeserving. This line of thinking is common in our society. I'd guess that 70 to 80 percent of individuals have feelings of not being good enough. Where does this low self-esteem come from? You guessed it—our programming. For most of us, it comes from hearing 20 more "You're doing it wrongs" for every "You're doing it right." Ten "Stop talking so much" for every two "You're a genius; tell me more." Even if our parents were supportive, many of us still end up with feelings of not being able to measure up to their expectations. Once again, we're not good enough.

To add to this programming, most of us grew up with the principle of punishment in our lives. This means that if you do something wrong, you will be punished. Some of us were punished by our parents, teachers, or some other authority figure in our lives. Our school system plays a big part in this programming. For example, if you make a mistake, you get a bad grade. For most people, the conditioning of punishment is ingrained in us, even as adults. Because there is no one around to punish them, when adults make a mistake, they subconsciously punish themselves. When we were young, this punishment may be in the form of, "You were bad, so no video games." Today, that conditioning can take the form of, "You were bad, so no money." This is how some people subconsciously self-sabotage their success and limit their earnings.

It all makes sense now why people have difficulty receiving. All you have to do is make one mistake, and you're doomed to carry the burden of poverty for the rest of your life. You're being way too harsh on yourself, don't you think? But since when did the mind become logical and compassionate? Again, your mind is a computer with folders, filled with past programming, made-up meanings, and stories of drama and disaster. Unfortunately, "making sense" isn't its strong suit.

Here's some good news: In the end, it doesn't matter whether you feel worthy or not. You can still be rich. There are plenty of wealthy people that don't feel immensely worthy. Some wealthy people even use it as motivation to get rich, to "prove themselves." The idea that self-worth is essential for net worth is exactly that — an idea — but it isn't necessarily true. As discussed earlier, getting rich to prove yourself may not make you happy, so you're better off creating wealth for other reasons. The important thing here is to realize that your feeling of unworthiness won't prevent you from getting rich, strictly financially. This could actually be a point of motivation.

Come to the realization that whether you are worthy or not is all a made-up "story." Nothing has meaning except for the meaning we give it. God didn't stamp you at birth as worthy or unworthy. There is no one that comes around and stamps you "worthy" or "unworthy." Only you can do that. You make it up. You create your reality with thought and determine if you're going to be worthy. It's all about perspective. If you say you're worthy, then you are worthy. If you say you're not worthy, well then, you're not worthy. Either way, you will live in the story that you decide. This is a critical point, so please read this paragraph again.

The question at hand is: Why would anyone do this to themselves? Why would anybody make up the story that they're not worthy? The simplest way to explain it is, that's just the nature of the human mind. It's the protective part of us that's always looking for what's wrong. Ever notice how a bird doesn't worry about these things? Could you imagine a bird saying, "I'm not going to collect many worms to eat this year to prepare for the flight down south, because I'm not worthy?" Even these low-intelligence creatures wouldn't subject themselves to this. Only the most advanced creatures on the planet, humans, have the ability to limit themselves like this.

Here's a suggestion: It's much easier to change your story, so change that instead of worrying about changing your worthiness. Simply make up a new story that is more supportive and live into that. It's a lot faster and more efficient. This new story has to come from you, because the old story of being unworthy isn't serving you. It doesn't make a difference what anyone says or has said in the past. You have to believe it and buy into it for it to have any effect. Stop buying into that "worthiness" or "unworthiness" story and start taking the actions you need to take to get rich!

Wealthy people work hard and believe it's completely fine to be well rewarded for their efforts and the massive value they provide others. Poor people work hard too, but due to their feelings of unworthiness, they believe that it isn't appropriate for them to be well rewarded for their efforts. This belief creates the perfect opportunity for them to be the "perfect victims." Of course, you can't be a "good" victim if you are well rewarded, right? Many poor people actually believe they are better people because they are poor. Somehow, they believe they are more pious, spiritual, or good. In reality, the only thing poor people "are", is poor. What good do you do for poor people by being one of them? Who do you help by being broke? Wouldn't it be more effective for you to create wealth for yourself and then really be an agent of change and help others from a place of strength? It's tough to effect change from a position of weakness, financially speaking.

After sharing this perspective with a relative, he told me, "For the first time, I finally got it. I just couldn't understand how to feel good about having a lot of money when others have so little. I get it now, and I can't believe how flawed my thinking was." He then decided that it was time for him to become rich and help others along the way. This wasn't a close relative, so a year or so had passed before I talked to him again. I got a message online from him telling me he's making 10 times what he used to earn and that he feels great about it. He has been sharing his new-found knowledge with anyone that would listen. It's an amazing feeling for him to be able to assist some of his friends and family who are struggling.

If you have ever had the desire to get rich, then that means you have the wherewithal to have a lot of money. If the mind can conceive it, it can achieve it. If you have the wherewithal to have a lot of money, then you should have it. Why? Because at the end of the day, we are extremely blessed to be living in a society where each person is rich in comparison to many other parts of the world.

Some people will never have the opportunity to have a lot of money. If you are one of the lucky people who have this ability — and you do have the ability or you wouldn't be reading this book — then use your wherewithal for all its worth. Get super rich and help people who don't have the opportunity you do. This option makes much more sense to me than being broke and helping no one.

If you're one of the people who say, "If I get rich, money will change me. I don't want to be greedy and mean to people," this is just another justification for failure. Money will only make you more of what you already are. If you're kind, money will afford you opportunity to be kinder. If you're mean, money will afford you more opportunity to be mean. If you're generous, more money will allow you the opportunity to be more generous. Anyone that tells you different is more than likely broke!

In order to become a good receiver, you must begin to nurture yourself. Because we are creatures of habit, you will have to consciously practice receiving the best life has to offer. As discussed in a previous chapter, the "fun money" account comes into play here. This will help you validate your worthiness and strengthen your "receiving muscle."

Second, I want you to practice having extreme excitement and gratitude anytime you find or receive any money. When I was broke, I would never stoop down and pick up change when I saw it on the ground. I would let the cashier keep the change. Now that I'm wealthy, however, I pick up all things shiny that even remotely resembles money. I then thank God for His many blessings. I tell myself that this is only a sign that even more money is on the way! I don't concern myself much with the denomination because money is money, and finding money is a blessing. Now that I'm open and willing to receive everything that comes my way, I do just that!

Being open and willing to receive is absolutely critical in the creation of wealth. It's also critical if you plan on keeping it. Even if you are a poor receiver and you somehow fall into a large amount of money, it will most likely be gone quickly. Remember from earlier: "First the inner, then the outer." Once you expand your receiving "box," watch the money comes in to fill it like the rain filled the bucket. The universe abhors a vacuum. This saying means an empty space will always be filled. Ever notice what happens with an empty garage? It gets filled with junk over a relatively short period of time and usually doesn't stay empty for long. Once you expand your capacity to receive, you will.

As if your life won't already be better just by doing this, also, the rest of your life will open up. Not only will you receive more money, but you will also receive more joy, more love, more happiness, and more overall fulfillment. The way you are in one area is usually how you are in other areas as well. If you've been blocking yourself from receiving money, there's a good chance you've been blocking yourself from receiving other good things in life. The mind has a habit of over-generalizing. If you're a poor receiver, you're a poor receiver in all areas. The silver lining in all of this is that when you become an excellent receiver, you will be an excellent receiver everywhere. You will be open and willing to receive all that God has to offer in all areas of your life. Just remember to always keep saying, "Thank you" and showing gratitude as you receive all of your blessings.

Millionaire Mind Shift Action Items

Practice being a good receiver.

- Say, "Thank you" when someone compliments you. Do not return the compliment. This will allow you to fully receive the compliment.

Thank God for any money you find or receive.

Pamper yourself or do something special every month to nurture yourself. Do things that make you feel rich while doing them.

Start a "Birthday Club" with your family and/or friends. Everybody will give each other a predetermined amount of money on their birthday. This will increase the "receiving" muscle for more money to flow into your life.

Millionaire Mind Shift #6
Opportunities and Solutions

Wealthy people see opportunities. Poor people see problems. Wealthy people see potential for growth. Poor people see potential for loss. Wealthy people focus on rewards. Poor people focus on risks. I'm sure you've been asked by someone in your life, "Is the glass half full or half empty?" Your response to this question would determine whether you are a positive or negative thinker. For this discussion, this is more about your habitual perspective on the world. In most cases, poor people make their choices and decisions based on fear. Their minds are non-stop watching for what is wrong or what could go wrong in any situation. Their primary thought process is, "What if it doesn't work?" or "It won't work." Remember that we will attract into our lives whatever we focus our minds on. The middle-class people are a bit more optimistic, and their thought process is, "I hope this works."

Wealthy and successful people, on the other hand, take responsibility for the results in their lives and believe, "It will work." Successful people expect for things to work out and to win. They are confident in their abilities and creativity, and they believe that if they lose it all, they can find another way to succeed. For the most part, the higher the reward, the higher the risk. Successful people are willing to take a risk because they constantly see opportunity. They believe they can always make their money back, no matter what.

Poor people typically expect to fail. They lack the confidence in themselves and their abilities to navigate the money game. Poor people believe that it would be catastrophic if things don't work out as planned, and because all they see are problems, they are usually unwilling to take a risk. No risk, no reward.

To be clear: The willingness to take a risk does not necessarily mean that you are willing to lose. Wealthy people take educated and well-calculated risks. This isn't gambling or throwing spaghetti against the wall to see what sticks. Taking educated, well-calculated risks means that they research, do their due diligence, and make decisions based on facts. Wealthy people don't get stuck in "analysis paralysis," either. They do what they can in as short a time as possible, and then they make an informed decision to move forward or not.

While some poor people may claim to be preparing for an opportunity, it's really just a form of stalling. They're scared to death to make a play, going back and forth for weeks, even months, or possibly years on end, and by then the opportunity has passed. To make it worse, they often miss out on several other opportunities while they're "analyzing" the two-year-old opportunity. They will then rationalize the situation by saying, "Well I was getting ready." While they were "getting ready," the rich guy got in, made a fortune, and got out.

Some people believe that there is a certain element of "luck" associated with getting creating wealth and being successful. Of course, because I value self-responsibility, I believe it to a certain extent. In basketball, it might be the opposing team's player taking too many steps while dribbling, causing a turnover with 28 seconds on the clock, allowing your team to win the game. In a race, it could be a missed gear by your opponent that allows you to win by a bumper. In business, how many times have you heard of someone creating an app that's later bought for some crazy amount? This investor then gets rich. So, is he a business genius or is it sheer luck? My guess is that it's a bit of both.

The point here is that no luck will come your way unless you take some form of action. In order to succeed financially, you have to do something, start something, or buy something. When you do this, I believe God or a higher power will support you in miraculous ways for having the commitment and courage to make a move. Some will view it as luck, but at the end of the day, who cares what it is, really. It happens!

Another principle is at work here: Successful people focus on what they want, while poor people focus on what they don't want. Because wealthy people focus on opportunities in everything, lots of doors are opened for them. Their biggest problem now is handling all of the moneymaking possibilities they see and developing the clarity to say no to certain things. On the flipside, because poor people focus on the problem in everything, their biggest problem is handling all of the incredible problems they see.

It's simple. What you focus on is what you find in life. Focus on opportunities, and low and behold, that's what you find. Focus on problems, and dang it, that's exactly what you will find. By no means am I saying you shouldn't take care of problems. Of course, handle the problems that arise, but be sure to keep your goal in mind and keep moving toward the target. Keep your focus, using all of your time and energy to create what you want. When problems pop up like they often do, handle them, then quickly shift your focus back to your vision. Do not make your life about solving problems and putting out fires. Living in this way actually moves you backward. Spend your time and energy in thought and action when necessary, always moving toward your goal.

If you want to be wealthy and create financial freedom, I have very simple advice for you: Focus on making, keeping, and investing your money. If you want to be poor, focus on spending your money. You can read 100 books or take 100 courses on success, but you won't get around it. What you focus on you attract. If you focus on spending, you will attract more situations to spend.

Wealthy and successful people also understand that you will never know all the information before jumping into something. In business there is a saying, "Ready, fire, aim." This means that successful people get ready the best they can in as short a time as possible, take action, and correct along the way. It's insane to believe you can know everything that the future may hold and what may happen. It's flawed thinking to believe you can prepare for every possible circumstance that may happen someday and protect yourself from it.

The idea is to get in the game with whatever you've got, in whatever way you can. You just have to get the ball rolling in some way. For example, years ago I was planning on opening a car dealership in Memphis, Tennessee. I studied location options, the marketplace, and the auctions I needed to get signed up with to supply the cars. I also researched the kinds of cars and the price range that sold best in the area. So, I asked myself, "What would be the best way to really learn this business?" If you really want to learn a business, get into it, but you don't have to own it from Day 1. I could learn more about selling cars by actually doing it than by 10 years of research from the "outside."

So, that's exactly what I did. I got a job at Jim Keras Nissan. I experienced immediate success at the job because I'm a natural sales person. I made more money than I had ever made in my life, but the hours sucked! I was on a mission to learn the car business. I was grateful for the opportunity to learn it on someone else's dime and make six figures doing it.

I was the top sales person throughout my time at the car dealership. Because of this, I would talk with the managers as much as possible. Of course, they all liked me because I sold a lot of cars for them. I would chat with them about revenues, profits, and the other dealerships the owners had under their umbrella. I worked at the dealership for a little more than a year, until I had to return that one time (we discussed earlier in the book). I learned a lot about the car business, and I also learned that I did not want to own a dealership. Mission accomplished!

This is what I meant by "get in the game." It means entering the arena where you want to be in the future in any capacity, just to get started. This is by far the best way to learn about a business because you get to see it from the inside. Second, you are able to make the contacts you need, which may have been difficult to do from the outside. Third, once you're in the game, many other doors of opportunity may open for you. Once you're on the inside and see what's going on, you may discover a niche for yourself that you hadn't recognized before. Fourth, you may find that you don't really like the field, like me. Thank goodness I found that out before I got in too deep!

After spending a year or so in the car business, I had made more money than I had ever made in my life. I was saving more money than I ever had as well. While working at the dealership, I had a coworker who became my mentor in a completely unrelated business. He worked at the dealership simply because he liked talking to people and selling cars, but he didn't have to. He was a business owner, and he took me in under his wing and taught me the entire business. If I would not have "got in the game" by getting a job selling cars, I would not have been presented with the business opportunity that fit me better than owning a car dealership. The moral of the story is simple: Get in the game, because you never know what doors will open.

This shows that action always beats inaction. Successful people get started, and they trust that once they get in the game, they can make intelligent decisions in the present moment, make adjustments, and correct their path along the way. Poor people don't trust themselves or their abilities, so they think they have to know every single detail in advance, which is virtually impossible. Meanwhile, they end up doing absolutely nothing! In the end, wealthy people take action and usually win. Poor people, by telling themselves, "I'm not doing anything until I've identified every possible problem and know exactly what to do about it," never take action and unfortunately always lose. Wealthy people see an opportunity and jump on it, while poor people are still getting ready to attempt to jump.

Getting wealthy is not a stroll in the park. It is a journey full of obstacles, ups and downs, dead ends, turnarounds, and detours. Because the road to wealth is not a straight path as most would hope, most people don't take it. Most people don't want all of the new problems that come along with the responsibilities of creating wealth. This is the biggest difference between rich people and poor people. Wealthy and successful people are solution-oriented and are bigger than their problems. They spend their time and energy strategizing and coming up with answers to challenges that arise. They also create systems to make sure the problem doesn't occur again.

Poor, unsuccessful people shrink away from their problems and are problem-oriented. They spend their time and energy complaining and whining about the problem and rarely come up with any creative solutions to the problem. In most cases, poor people will do almost anything to avoid problems entirely. When they see a challenge, they turn and run. The funny thing about this behavior is that in their attempt to not have problems, they actually attract more problems. Why? Their focus is on problems and not solutions. The secret to success is not to avoid or shrink from your problems, but to grow yourself so you are bigger than any problem. How do you grow yourself? You grow yourself by focusing on solutions when faced with problems.

On a scale of one to 10, imagine a level 2 person being faced with a level 3 problem. This problem would seem like a big problem from the perspective of the level 2 person. At this point, the level 2 person has one of two options: This level 2 person can decide that the problem is too big and not deal with the problem, or the level 2 person can focus on finding a solution to the problem. With a little bit of focus, this level 2 person would be able to overcome the level 3 problem.

Now imagine this same person has grown themselves to a level 8 person. At this point, would that same level 3 problem be a big problem or a little problem? The exact same problem would now be a little problem. As you grow yourself to a level 10 person, a level 8 problem won't even register in your brain as a "problem" anymore. It's just a normal occurrence for the level 10 person to handle, like maneuvering traffic during rush hour.

Here's the thing about problems: Whether you are rich or poor, you will always have problems and obstacles in your life as long as you live. The problem is never the issue, though. Your ability to focus on solutions is what matters most. If you have a big problem in your life, that means you are being a small person. Keep in mind that the outer world you experience is only a reflection of what's going on inside. If you want to make permanent change in your life, stop focusing on the size of your problem, and start focusing on solutions. As you focus on solutions, you will attract more solutions, and in turn you will become a bigger person with each problem you overcome. Make the decision now to be a bigger person and not allow any problem or obstacle to take away from your happiness or success.

As you become a bigger person, the bigger the problems you can handle, the bigger the business you can handle. The more money you can save, the more money you can handle. The more money you can handle, the more investment opportunities you can handle. The more investments you can handle, the more wealth you can handle. Your wealth can only grow to the extent that you grow. The objective is to grow to be a big enough person that you can overcome any problem or obstacle that gets in the way of you creating wealth and keeping it once you have it.

The ability to hang on to your wealth is a whole other world, by the way. I found this out the hard way as I proceeded to lose my first $1 million over a relatively short period of time. I was under the illusion that once you made it, you made it! I was in for a rude awakening, as the reality of super high income with no assets, with an insane spending habit, collided. In hindsight, I know exactly what my issue was. At that point in my life, my "toolbox" wasn't quite big enough to hold the wealth I had achieved. Thank God I learned the exact same principles in this book that you are learning now, so I was able to recondition myself. Not only did I make that $1 million back, but I've also made millions more since. Best of all, I have assets now that keep growing at phenomenal rates. I didn't understand how to invest my money, which was a problem that required me to grow in order to overcome.

To put this into perspective, think of yourself as a container for wealth. If your container for wealth is small and your money is big, you will lose it. Your container will overflow just like a bucket filled to the top with water. The spillage can be equated to frivolous spending or bad investments. You simply cannot have more money than your container can handle. You must grow to be a big container so you can create and attract even more wealth. Remember earlier when we discussed how the universe abhors a vacuum? If you are a large container, wealth will rush in to fill the space.

The bottom line is that if you become a master at handling problems and become solution-oriented, nothing can stop you from success. You will become unstoppable! And when you become unstoppable, anything and everything is available to you. Simply choose it and it is yours!

Millionaire Mind Shift Action Items

Get in the game.

- Work for or partner with someone to learn the ropes.

Practice optimism.

Focus on what you have and not on the lack thereof. Make a list of 10 things you are grateful for. Appreciate what you've got, and you will get more.

Pay close attention to how you react to problems. Gently remind yourself that you are solution-oriented, and start focusing on the solution instead of the problem.

When faced with a problem:

- Write the problem at the top of a blank piece of paper.
- List 10 actions you can take to resolve or improve the situation.

Millionaire Mind Shift #7
Promote Yourself and Your Value

We've all been suckered into a "free seminar" that is usually just a big sales pitch about other courses and offers that actually cost. If you've never experienced this, take it from me, it is extremely entertaining to "people watch" at events like this. As mentioned earlier, I've always been an avid learner, so I've been to my fair share of seminars on a vast array of subjects. The reactions are always interesting to me.

Most of the people in the audience are excited and appreciate the opportunity to hear what other courses are offered. Then you have the people who are there for what they can get for free, and, "How dare you try to sell me something!?" is screaming from their body language and facial expressions. They resent any promotion, regardless of the benefits for them. If the latter example sounds anything like you, it's important to realize this characteristic about yourself.

The resentment of promotion is one of the greatest obstacles to success. In most cases, people who have an issue with promotion and being sold to are usually not doing so well financially. If you aren't willing to let people know that you, your product, or your service exists, how can you create a large income in your own business or as a representative of a business? This goes for employees as well as business owners. As an employee, if you are not willing to promote your qualities, someone who is willing will bypass you in climbing the corporate ladder.

Most people have a problem with promotions or sales for several reasons. One reason may be that you have had a bad experience in the past with people promoting to you inappropriately. Maybe you perceived their approach as a "hard sell" on you. Maybe they approached you at an inopportune time, or maybe they just wouldn't take no for an answer. Realize that this experience is in the past, and holding on to it may not be serving you in the best way today.

Next, you may have had a less than great experience when you tried to sell something to someone and that person shut you down completely. In this situation, your dislike for promotion is simply a projection of your own fear of rejection. Even in this scenario, realize that the past does not necessarily equal the future.

Third, many of us were conditioned when we were young that it was frowned upon to "toot your own horn." When it comes to business and money, if you don't toot your own horn, nobody will. This is how it works in the real world. Wealthy and successful people are always willing to promote their qualities and value to anyone who will listen to hopefully end up doing business with them.

Lastly, some people feel that promotion is simply beneath them. This is what I like to call the "big ole me, lil' ole you" syndrome, otherwise known as the "I'm too good for that" attitude. The flawed thinking behind this behavior is that if people want what you have, they should somehow find you in the millions of people on the web and come to you. People with this belief are either broke or on their way to being so. They can hope that the people who need their product or service will scour the internet and social media sites for them, but the reality is that the marketplace is crowded with products and services. Even if their product or service is the best, no one will ever know because they're "too good" to tell anyone.

Wealthy and successful people are almost always excellent promoters. They are always willing to promote their products, services, and ideas with enthusiasm and passion. They're able to package and present themselves in a way that's extremely attractive to all. Think of the well-groomed salesman and the nice lady at the counter who looks like she could model for a living. Both examples are nothing more than "packaging."

Think of Puff Daddy, for example. He's reinvented, or should I say repackaged, himself several times over the last couple of decades. At the time of writing he goes by Diddy, but either way, this guy is the textbook example. He is always promoting whatever it is that he is involved in, whether it be, music, television, liquor, or clothing. Good luck on trying to get him to not mention one of his many offerings every chance he gets!

Generally speaking, wealthy people are leaders, and in my experience, all great leaders are great promoters. In order to be a great leader, you must have followers and supports. It's like John Maxwell says: "If you're a leader and no one is following, then you're only taking a walk." To be a leader, you have to be able to sell, inspire, and motivate people to buy into your vision. The CEO of a company has to sell his ideas to his C-level executives, then the C-level executive sells the ideas to the management team, and so on. The CEO actually even has to sell himself first! Selling and getting rich go hand in hand. Even as a parent, you are selling your kids on eating their veggies and brushing their teeth. Any leader who can't or won't promote will most likely not be a leader for very long, whether it's at home, work, politics, business, sports, or even as a parent. I really want to drive this point home: Leaders earn a lot more than followers!

The main point here isn't whether or not you like to promote. You have to understand why you are promoting. What are your beliefs?

Do you really believe in what you are offering? Do you really believe in the value that you add? Do you believe in the product or service? If you truly believe in your value, how could you possibly hide it from the people who need it? Suppose the whole world was shut down due to Coronavirus, and you had a cure for it. Would you hide it from the world? Would you wait for someone to read your mind and or guess that you have a cure? Now, to turn it around, what would you think of someone who didn't offer a suffering country their cure because they were too shy, afraid, or cool to promote it?

Typically, people who have a problem with promotion don't fully believe in themselves or in their product. As a result, it's difficult for them to imagine that other people can believe in them or the product enough to actually buy in. If you believe in what you are offering, then it is your duty and obligation to let as many people know about it as possible. In this way, you not only help people, but you also get rich!

Millionaire Mind Shift Action Items

Read books, listen to podcasts and audio books, watch videos, and take courses on emotional intelligence, marketing, sales, and human nature.

Rate yourself from one to 10 in terms of how much you believe in yourself, your product/service, or your future product/service. If you don't believe in what you are offering, start representing something you truly believe in.

Millionaire Mind Shift #8
Think Big, Think Both

If you were to ask the most successful people in the world how they went from below a $1 million-dollar net worth to as high as a $1 billion-dollar-plus net worth, they would tell you that the secret is to think big. There are four main factors that determine your value in the marketplace: supply, demand, quality, and quantity. Most people have heard of supply and demand, which are very important. For this discussion, though, we will focus on the quantity factor. The quantity factor is the measure of how much value you deliver to the marketplace. Another way to say this is, how many people do you actually serve or affect?

In one of my businesses, for instance, we operate in five different states and nine counties. When we first started, we were in only one market, which was our local market. By hiring consultants, we were able to grow the business to nine markets within a year. Is there a difference in income from serving one market versus serving nine markets? You better believe it! Take a look at the network marketing business. Do you think there is a difference between someone who has 10 people in their down-line and someone who has 1,000 people? Definitely!

How do you want to live your life? How do you want to play the game of money? Are you going to step of to the big leagues or are you going to stay on the pewee team? Will you play big or choose to play small? It's totally up to you. Most people choose to play small, mainly because of fear. They are scared halfway to death of failing and they are even more afraid of success. People also play small because they feel unworthy, as we discussed earlier. They don't feel that they are good enough or important enough to make a real difference in people's lives.

I hate to burst your little selfish bubble, but your life is not just about you. Life is about contributing to others and adding value. It's about aligning with and living your true mission and purpose for being here on this earth. It's all about adding your unique puzzle to world. The world needs what you have to offer. Most people are so stuck in their own heads and weighed down by their egos that everything revolves around me, me, and more me. If you want to be rich in the truest sense, it can't be all about you. You have to add value to other people's lives.

We were each blessed with natural talents — things that we are naturally good at. These gifts were given to you for a reason, which is to use and share with others. Research on the happiest people shows that they use their natural talent to its utmost capacity. Part of your mission in life should be to share your gifts and value with as many people as possible. You have to play big in order to do this.

I'm an entrepreneur and a salesman naturally. The definition of an entrepreneur, according to Dictionary.com, is a person who organizes and manages any enterprise, especially a business, usually with considerable initiative and risk. I actually like to break it down even further to a simpler definition. An entrepreneur is nothing more than a problem solver. Whether you are a full-time entrepreneur or work full time with a side business, I have a question for you: Would you rather solve problems for more people or fewer people? If you replied more, which I hope you did, you need to start thinking bigger and decide to help lots of people. The byproduct of thinking big is that the more people you help, the richer you become in all areas of your life: mentally, emotionally, spiritually, and most definitely financially.

Every single person on this planet was put here for a mission. We all have a purpose if we are breathing, and we are here for a reason. You will know when you have completed your mission, and that will be when you are no longer breathing. Until then, your community needs what you have, the country needs what you have, even the world needs what you have to offer. There are way too many people who are not doing their jobs and are not fulfilling their duty and obligations to others. There are too many people who are playing small and allowing their fear to rule them, preventing the full commitment required to GO BIG! The result is that far too many of us are not living up to our full potential. We owe ourselves more, and our contributions to others are needed. If not you, then who?

Every one of us has our own unique purpose for being here. Maybe you are a real estate investor who buys properties, renovates, and makes money from reselling the property to a homeowner. Maybe your strategy is to fix properties and rent them out for the cash flow and appreciation. Maybe you are a developer who builds houses from the ground up. Regardless of which of the many strategies you choose, what matters is what your mission is. How are you helping? You add value to your community by revitalizing communities and helping families find affordable housing they may not otherwise be able to find. In order to think big, the question is: How many people do you want to affect? Is your goal to help 10, 20, or 1,000 families? This is the essence of thinking big.

As the world becomes more interconnected and we are a part of a global economy, there is more opportunity than ever to go big. The world doesn't need more people playing small. It's time to step up and create generational wealth for your family. It's time to start sharing your gifts instead of hoarding them. It's time for you to start playing the game of life to win big. Small thinking leads to small actions, which in the end leads to being broke and unfulfilled. Thinking BIG leads to BIG ACTIONS, which leads to having BIG money and BIG meaning. The choice is yours!

Because wealthy and successful people think big, they live in a world of abundance. Poor people live in a world of limitations. While of course, both live in the same physical world, the difference is in their perspective. In most cases, poor and middle-class people come from a scarcity mindset. You can recognize this mindset when they say things like, "There's only so much to go around," "There's never enough," and "Can't win for losing," or they say my favorite, "You can't have your cake and eat it, too." Of course, you may not be able to physically have everything in the world, however I do believe you can have everything you really want.

Do you want to build an amazing business or raise a family? Wealthy and successful people do both. Do you want a successful career or to work from home? Both! Do you want to be rich or happy? Both! Do you want to work in your passion or make a fortune? Both! Do you want to have fun or make real progress in life? Both! Poor people, more often than not, choose one over the other.

Wealthy and successful people understand that with using a little creativity, finding solutions, and thinking big, they can almost always figure out a way to have the best of both worlds. The next time you are faced with an either/or situation, I want you to ask yourself a question: "How can I have both?" By asking this question, you will change your life. You will go from scarcity and limitation to possibilities and abundance!

Please don't limit your thinking of "both" to only material things. One of my mottos in real estate is to create a win/win situation. We attempt to buy the property from a distressed seller for a fair price, pay our contractors a fair price to complete the work, and then finally resell the property on the open market just a tad below market value so it's a "win" for our end buyer as well. In my younger days in business, I approached situations and negotiations with the goal of making my point and making sure I don't pay one cent more than I planned to. I would go into the discussion thinking, "Either they win or I win." Even though I would sometimes win by this approach, in the end it definitely cost me future business with certain suppliers, and sometimes ended in heated arguments.

However, today I have trained myself to only think in terms of "both." I approach all discussions completely openly and am willing to create a situation that will work for all parties involved. We are going to both state what we want, and we will find some middle ground we both can live with. My goal is to have both!

Here's another example: A few years back, I decided to sell my primary residence and start renting homes. My wife and I kept a close eye on the available rentals in the areas where we preferred to live, and we were told by leasing agents that what we were looking for usually gets snapped up really quick. The market for higher-end rentals was slim in the city where we lived. We were told that we would need to buy in order to get the amenities we wanted, and it would cost at least a half million. My intention was to clear my personal credit of a mortgage to invest more into income-producing properties and to find a rental comparable to my current home. Most people would either lower their expectations or buy another home. I held out for both. We moved into a newly constructed home with every single amenity we wanted at the time. This is the power of thinking "both"!

I always told my parents that I would be rich one day and that I wouldn't have to work the rest of my life. Their response was something along the lines of, "If a man doesn't work, he doesn't eat." They said, "You get a good job and stick with it until you can retire, and then you go see the world." Their view on life was that you take care of making a living first, then if there's time left over, enjoy your life. I remember thinking to myself, "If I listen to them, I'll end up just like them." Was my journey to creating wealth tough? Yes, of course! I touched on this earlier, but even though there were times I worked a job I hated just so I could eat once per day and pay my rent, I never lost my intention to always "think both." I never got stuck long-term in a job or business that I didn't like. I kept my main goal in mind at all times.

There is no subject in which it's more important to "think both" than in the subject of money. Most poor and middle-class people believe they have to make a choice between money and other aspects in life. As a result, they rationalize to themselves that money is not that important in comparison to other things. Money is extremely important, and to say that it isn't as important as something else in life is crazy. What's more important, your eyes or your hearing? Could it be that both your eyes and the ability to hear are important?

Money is a tool. Having enough of it will allow you to slide through life instead of just scraping by. It's a tool to buy your freedom — freedom to buy whatever you want and to live your life on your own terms. Money allows you to enjoy the finer things in life, while giving you the opportunity to help others. More importantly, money allows you to not have to spend your time and energy worrying about "not having money." Most poor and middle-class people's argument at this point is, "Happiness is important, too." Happiness is absolutely important, too, but this is where most get it confused. Many people believe that both happiness and being rich cannot coexist. Again, this is nothing more than "poor programming" at play. People who are rich in every sense of the word understand very well that you have to have both! Just as you need both your arms and legs, you need both money and happiness.

Not thinking "both" may also trip people who believe that their having more results in someone else having less. Again, this can be attributed to self-sabotaging and fear-based programming. The idea that wealthy people are hoarding all of the money and that's why you're poor is ludicrous. This shows an assumption that there is a limited supply of money. I'm not an economist, but I do know that they just keep printing this stuff. At the time of writing, the US is in a pandemic, and the US Treasury printed more than a trillion bucks! Actually, what most people don't know is that this paper we call money hasn't been tied to any real asset since the '70s! So even if the wealthy had all the money today, there will be millions, if not billions, being printed very soon.

The other thing most people with this scared mindset don't realize is that the same money can be used over and over. Let's look at an example with five people standing in a circle, with each person representing a different type of business. The first person buys a pen from the second person for $5. Now person number two has made a sale and now has $5. That second person then turns and buys a pack of paper from the third person. Then the third person will take the $5 and buy a water bottle and so on. As you can see, the same $5 was used to bring value to each person who had it. That same $5 went through five people's hands and created $5 worth of value for each, but $25 in value to the economy. The money doesn't get depleted as it is circled around. The more money you have, the more money you have to put into the circle, which means more people have more money to trade for even more value!

When you have money, and use it, you and the person who you spend the money with both have value. If you're so worried about other people getting their "fair share," as if there were a share, get as rich as possible so you can spread the money around. I strongly encourage you to do away with the myth that money is in any way bad if you are wealthy. If you really want to live a life without limits, embrace thinking "both" and let go of everything else.

Millionaire Mind Shift Action Items

List your natural talents and how you can put them to use in your personal and work life.

Brainstorm with a group of people how you can solve problems for 10 times the people you affect in your job or business.

Practice thinking "both" anytime you're presented with alternatives.

Be a role model for others by thinking big and thinking "both."

Millionaire Mind Shift #9
Take Action in Fear

In Part One of this book, we discussed the process of manifestation. Thoughts lead to feelings, feelings lead to actions, and actions lead to results. Lots of people "think" about getting rich while doing affirmations, visualizations, and meditations. I'm a big fan of meditation, and I meditate on average two to three times per day in 15-minute increments. To this day, a big bag of money has never fallen in my lap while I've been meditating, but there is always an action part to manifestations, and this is something I think a lot of people miss. Reciting affirmations, meditating, and making vision boards are all great tools, but none of those things will bring you real money in the real world on their own. In the real world, you have to take action to become a financial success. I learned about the Law of Attraction and manifestations, and I struggled with them for almost 10 years before I could get it to be my way of living my life. It's the action that makes the difference.

Why is action critical in the manifestation process? Our thoughts and feelings are a part of our inner world. Our results are found on the outside because our outer world is a reflection of what's going on inside. That means that action is the "bridge," in a sense, between your inner world and outer world. You don't want to just take action for action's sake. You should take inspired action. To really understand the manifestation process at a deeper level is beyond the scope of this book, but action is extremely important nonetheless.

So, what is it that prevents us from taking actions we know we need to take? It's fear! Fear of the unknown, doubt, and worry about the future are just a few of the greatest obstacles to success and happiness in life. Another one of the biggest differences between rich people and poor people is that rich people are willing to act regardless of fear. In most cases, poor people will let fear stop them dead in their tracks. One of the biggest pitfalls most people make is waiting for the feeling of fear to die down or go away completely before they are willing to make a move. These people usually wait forever and sit on the sidelines their entire life. You have to learn to "tame the beast within." Fear is your mind trying to keep you safe in your comfort zone. Notice that I used the word "tame" instead of "kill" the beast within. Don't run from the beast, don't get rid of the beast—tame the beast within.

It is not necessary for you to get rid of fear in order to succeed. Wealthy and successful people have fear, doubts, and worries, too. They just don't allow these feelings to stop them from being a financial success. On the other hand, unsuccessful people experience the same emotions, but they let those feelings stop them. Because we are creatures of habit, you can practice acting without fear. For example, you need to practice acting in spite of doubt, worry, uncertainty, inconvenience, and discomfort. All of these things will build your muscle for acting without fear.

I have people approach me all the time and ask what their first investment should be. My reply is always that your first investment should be in yourself. Do this by reading as many books as possible. The response that I get in most cases is, "Oh, I don't like to read" or something to that effect. If you will let reading a book stop you from doing something you need and want to do, then anything and everything else will stop you, too. You can only be one of two types of person. You are either a person who can be stopped or a person who can't be stopped. It's your choice. If you want to create wealth for your family and have the ability to help people, or to achieve another type of success, you have to be relentless! You have to be willing to do whatever it takes. You do this by training yourself to act without fear. Raise your hand in the meeting and give your opinion, even if it makes your palms sweat. Try it and see how empowered you feel. Eventually you will look for opportunities to feel uncomfortable and push through. Each instance of this is an exercise to build your muscle to be unstoppable!

Remember, the road to creating wealth is not always convenient. Getting rich is not always easy, and it can be extremely challenging at times. But at the end of the day, so what? Being broke is pretty hard, too. In life, I believe that if you are willing to do what is hard, you will have a much easier time while trying to grow your life. But if you only want to do what is easy in life and stay within your comfort zone, life will be hard. Wealthy and successful people don't live their life based on what's easy and convenient. Waking up and going to work every day, living the same year over and over each year for 40 years, is easy and convenient.

We have to also be able to take action despite discomfort. The most sought-after word in the middle-class dictionary is "comfortable." Comfortable is where you are right now. If you want to rise to a new level in life, you have to break out of your comfort zone. That's where all of the magic is happening! Practice doing things that make you feel uncomfortable. Most people are not willing to feel that way, especially on purpose. Because being "comfortable" is their biggest priority in life, they don't do much. I'll let you in a little secret: Being comfortable is highly overrated. Being "comfortable" may give you the warm and fuzzies at night, but it's impossible to grow as a person inside your comfort zone. In order to grow as a person, you must expand your comfort zone. The only time you're growing is when you're outside your comfort zone.

I'm sure you don't remember when you first started walking, but hopefully you have witnessed a child learning to walk. Actually, we can learn a lot by observing children and their limitless way of thinking. It isn't until we get around school age that we start getting talked out of our dreams and programmed to fit into society's "box." But if you've seen a child learning to walk, you can relate to the example. I'm pretty sure that crawling and scooting around is a lot more comfortable. Does the child fall the first time and decide that walking isn't for them or that it's uncomfortable? Of course not. Everything is uncomfortable in the beginning, but if you hang in there, you will eventually move through the un-comfort zone and succeed. At that point, you will have leveled up as far as expanding your comfort zone, which means you are a "bigger" person who can handle more.

If you really want to create wealth and be successful, you'd better get comfortable with being uncomfortable. Consciously practice getting uncomfortable and doing what scares you. As you expand your comfort zone, you will expand your income and wealth. When you are willing to stretch yourself, you open yourself up to new opportunities that allow you to attract and hang on to more income and wealth. Wealthy and successful people have big comfort zones that are expanding daily.

To this day, I don't know of anyone who has ever died of discomfort. But living for the elusive "comfortable" status has killed more ideas, opportunities, actions, and growth than anything else. Comfort kills! So, flip it on its head and become a "comfort killer." If your primary goal in life is to be comfortable, I guarantee you will never be rich. You may disagree, but you will never be truly happy, either. Happiness doesn't come from living a "middle-of-the-road" kind of life, always wondering what could have happened. Happiness comes as a result of having the freedom to live on your own terms, be who you truly are, and live up to your fullest potential.

The next time you feel uncomfortable, notice and experience the feelings of discomfort, recognizing that they are just that—only feelings. Your feelings do not have the power to stop you. If you are willing to press through, regardless of discomfort, you will eventually reach your goal. It doesn't really matter if the discomfort ever goes away. In fact, when the discomfort does lessen, take that as a sign that you are headed in the right direction and really press in. Keep in mind that the minute you become comfortable, you stop growing. To grow yourself to your fullest potential, you must learn to thrive, living outside of your comfort zone. By doing so, you will quickly move to a higher level in life. Be sure to take some time to look at your bank account along the way as well, because that will be growing quickly too, no doubt.

Your mind is one of the greatest dream curators ever in history— even better than the writers for "reality" TV! Your mind makes up incredible stories that are usually based in fear, dramas, disasters, and a series of things that have never happened and most likely never will. Mark Twain once said, "I've had thousands of problems in my life, most of which never actually happened."

One extremely important thing you must understand about your mind is that you are not your mind. You are so much greater than your mind alone. Your mind is a part of you, just like your eyes are a part of you. By using the principles in this book, you must learn to control your conscious mind, manage it, and train it to work for you instead of against you. The training and management of your mind is one of the most beneficial skills to obtain in terms of both success and happiness in general.

So how do you train your mind? You start by simply observing how your mind consistently produces thoughts that are not supportive to your happiness and wealth creation. As you identify these thoughts floating by randomly, you can begin to consciously replace those non-empowering thoughts with thoughts that serve you better. You replace those thoughts with what you are learning in this book. Adopt these ways of thinking as your own. We don't need to have some big ceremony. Decide right now that your life will be better if you choose to have the Millionaire Mind Shift and do everything described in this book. The old way of self-defeating mental habits is over and done with. You have the power to choose your thoughts. You have the power to cancel any thought that is not supporting you at any time. You can instead install empowering thoughts at any given time, simply by shifting your focus. You have the power to control your mind.

Robert Allen once said, "No thought lives in your head rent-free." What that means is that your negative thoughts will cost you in the long run. You will pay in lost opportunities, energy, time, health, and ultimately, your level of happiness. If you want to move your life to the next level quickly, begin by dividing every thought into one of two categories: empowering or disempowering. Observe the thoughts you have throughout the day, and determine if they are supportive or non-supportive to your happiness and success. At that point, you have the option to choose to entertain only the empowering thoughts and refuse to focus on the disempowering ones. This will take some practice and getting used to. This goes further than simply positive thinking. This is power thinking. If you start doing this, your life will never be the same.

The difference between positive thinking and power thinking are slight, but important nonetheless. In my opinion, with positive thinking, people pretend things are peaches and cream when they don't really believe it. With power thinking, we understand that nothing has meaning except for the meaning we give it in this present moment, and we are making up the story and its meaning. With positive thinking, people believe their thoughts are true, whereas power thinking recognizes our thoughts are not true. Because we're making up a story anyway, you might as well make up a story that supports you. You do this because those thoughts are more useful, and honestly, they feel a lot better as well.

Millionaire Mind Shift Action Items

List your three greatest worries, concerns, or fears in regards to money. Then list the outcomes that would make you happy for each and focus on that anytime those concerns arise.

Make it a habit to get outside of your comfort zone. Compliment a stranger, speak to people you normally wouldn't speak to at work, raise your prices in your business, wake up an hour earlier to exercise, or go camping with no tent. Just do something that makes you uncomfortable.

Start using power thinking. Observe your thoughts and only entertain the ones that support your happiness and success.

Millionaire Mind Shift #10
Associate with Successful People

Oftentimes, poor people look at other people's success with resentment, jealousy, and envy, or they justify their lack of success by saying things like, "They're just lucky," or "I'm sure they're doing something illegal." What you have to realize is that if you view rich people as "bad" in any way and you want to be a "good" person, that means you can never be rich. You cannot be something you dislike or think is bad. The resentment toward rich people I have witnessed would lead you to believe that the rich people make them poor. "Rich people took all the money, so there's none left for me."

Most people think they don't resent the rich, but depending on your mood, falling into the trap can happen to anyone — admittedly even me. Recently I walked into my office, and my employees were in a huddle discussing the booking fees for several performing artists. Apparently, this list was released on social media and was not typically made available to the general public. They were discussing how this one particular artist has the highest booking fee per show. When they told me his booking fee, I heard myself say, "That is way too much for that guy to be getting paid per show. He's not even that good." I felt the negativity inside me, and I caught myself just in time. Here I am, Mr. Millionaire Mind Shift himself, actually resenting another entrepreneur. I immediately switched my thought to admiration: "You know what, good for him that he can get booked for that much. Hopefully one day I can be booked for doing something I love to do like he can." Remember, my opinions on the artist make no difference to his happiness or success, but they do make a difference to my happiness and wealth. Also keep in mind that thoughts and opinions are neither good nor bad, right nor wrong, but they can be empowering or disempowering to your happiness and success as they enter your life.

The moment I felt that negative energy, my inner alarms went crazy, and as I've trained myself to do, I immediately turned the thought around in my head and neutralized it. The good news is that you don't have to be perfect to get rich, but you must recognize when your thinking isn't empowering to yourself or others. Then, quickly refocus on more supportive thoughts. The more you study this book and apply it to your life, the faster and easier the process will be.

The fact is, resenting the rich is one of the best ways to stay broke. As discussed earlier, we are creatures of habit, and to overcome this habit, we need to practice. Instead of resenting rich people, I want you to practice admiring rich people and loving rich people. By doing this, when you become rich, other people will admire and love you as well. Our outer world is only a reflection of what's going on inside. One of the things I like to do is ask God to bless people who I come into contact with. If you see a person with a beautiful home, say, "Thank you, God, for blessing them with that home." If you see a person with a beautiful car, say, "Thank you, God, for their car and keep them safe." Bless others when they have the things you want.

Successful people also look at other successful people as a source of motivation. They see other successful people as models to learn from. They say things to themselves like, "If they can do it, I can do it, too." Modeling is one of the primary ways that people learn, which we learned earlier. Wealthy and successful people are extremely grateful that others have succeeded before them, so they now have a proven blueprint to follow. This will ultimately make it easier for them to attain their own success. This goes back to the age-old question of why you'd want to reinvent the wheel. There are proven methods for success and wealth that work for virtually everyone that applies them. Therefore, the fastest and easiest way to create wealth is to learn exactly how rich people play the money game. The goal here is to simply model their inner and outer strategies. If you have the exact same mindset and you take the exact same actions, there is a good chance you will get the exact same results. That's what I did. That's what this book is all about.

Unlike the rich, when poor people hear about other people's success, they often judge, criticize, and make fun of them. Do you know anybody like this? Do you have any family members like this? The question is: How can you learn from someone that you criticize and put down?

Whenever I'm introduced to successful people, I create a way to connect with them in some way. I want to talk to them, learn how they think, exchange contacts, and if we have common interests, possibly become personal friends with them. If you're thinking that I'm wrong for preferring to be friends with rich people, think of it this way: As I've mentioned before, energy is contagious, and I prefer the energy of the successful.

So, what happens if you're positive and want to grow, but your spouse/partner is a "Debby Downer"? What if the people I'm closest to aren't into personal growth and make fun of me for it? Do you leave them? Do you try to change them? My advice is to not bother trying to change negative people. That's not your job. Your job is to learn what you're learning to better yourself and your life. Be the model for them, and maybe they'll see the light in you and want some of it. Energy is contagious, and darkness dissipates in the light. Someone would have to work really hard to stay in a "dark" place when you are a source of light around them. All you have to do is be the best version of yourself. If they choose to ask your secret, then tell them. Everything happens for a reason, and that reason is there to assist you. Sure, it's a lot more difficult to be positive around people and circumstances that are negative, but that's your test! Just as "iron sharpens iron," if you stay true to what you are learning and your values, you will grow faster and sharper, regardless if others around you are full of doubt.

You make the decision each day to either affect or infect people. The same is true for everyone else—either they affect you or infect you. Would you hug and kiss a person who you knew had the Coronavirus? Most people would say no. From now on, look at negative thinking as "Coronavirus of the Mind." Negativity will eat away at you on the inside, just like the Coronavirus. Do you want to be around people like that?

The saying, "birds of a feather flock together" holds true here. Were you aware that most people earn within 20 percent of the average income of their closest friends? That's why it is imperative for you to watch the associates you choose to spend your time with. From my experience, wealthy people don't only join the country club to play golf. They join to connect with other wealthy and successful people. If you want to fly with the eagles, don't hang around with the chickens. I make it a point to only associate with positive and successful people. I disassociate myself as much as I can from negative people, which is just as important.

I also make it a point to remove myself from toxic situations. There is no reason to infect myself with bad energy, which includes arguing, gossiping, and other similar behaviors. I also group watching mindless TV in here as well, because it's all based in negativity and drama. In my opinion, it's okay to watch that sort of TV if it's purpose is solely for entertainment. For example, I rarely watch TV and I am not a sports fan, but I do watch the highlights on ESPN during basketball season. I enjoy seeing professionals' career highlights, and I enjoy listening to their mindset in the interviews. I love to hear the mindset of champions. In my opinion, anyone who is a professional athlete is a champion. They have outcompeted tens of thousands of other players to get there. When they win, they say things like, "It was a great effort from our team." When they lose, they say things like, "This was only one game, we'll be back and do whatever it takes to win the next time."

Successful people hang around with winners, while unsuccessful people hang around with people that are, well, unsuccessful. Why? It's simply a matter of comfort. Wealthy and successful people are comfortable with other successful people. They feel like they are worthy of being around them. Some poor people are uncomfortable with highly successful people. They either have a fear of rejection or feel as though they don't belong. The ego then tries to protect itself and goes into judgment and criticism mode.

If your goal is to be wealthy and successful, you will have to change your inner blueprint to fully believe you are as good as any millionaire or multimillionaire that exists. A millionaire is no better or different from you, and until you understand that, getting rich will be difficult. It's a choice that you decide, and then it is done. It's all about deciding that you are just as good and then starting to act like it. Instead of resenting rich people, model them. Instead of shying away from rich people, stick your hand out and get to know them. If they can do it, you can do it.

Millionaire Mind Shift Action Items

Practice blessing what you want. Bless the people who you admire (or should admire).

Send a message to someone you know who is highly successful in any area to tell them how much you admire them for their achievements.

Read or watch a biography of someone who was extremely successful and use their story for inspiration, learning, and success strategies. Copy their mindset.

Mingle with rich people at the nicest hotels and restaurants in your city. Notice that the patrons are no different from you.

Identify the "Debby Downers" in your life and remove yourself from the situation or association. If it's family, you can choose to be around them less.

Stop watching mindless TV and the local news.

Millionaire Mind Shift #11
Lifelong Learner

For some odd reason, most poor people are often trying to prove that they're right. They put on a front as if they've got it all figured out, and it's just bad luck that has them broke and struggling. They say things like, "I already know that," for example. How do you know if you actually know something? The answer is simple: If you live it, then you know it. Anything other than that, you heard about it, read about it, but you definitely don't know it. To be blunt, if you're not really happy and really wealthy, there's most likely some things you have to learn about money, success, and life. As discussed earlier in the book, during my "car sales" days, I was fortunate enough to get advice from a multimillionaire client. "If you're not doing as well as you'd like, all that means is there's something you don't know." Fortunately, because of this, I went from a "know-it-all" to a "learn-it-all." Everything in my life changed from that point forward.

You can be right or you can be rich. Being "right" means you have to hold on to your old ways of thinking and approaching life. Unfortunately, it's those exact ways that have you where you are right now. This philosophy also goes for happiness in that you can be right or you can be happy. Think of it this way: You already know "your" way, so what you need is to know some new ways. That is the purpose of me writing this book. My goal is to give you some mental mind shifts that will help propel you toward success. New thoughts mean new actions, which will produce new results. This is why it is so important for you to always continue to learn and grow.

Nothing in this world is static. Everything that is alive is constantly changing. Where did we get the notion that learning ends after formal education? Take a plant, for example. If a plant is not growing, then it is dying. The same goes for us humans. If you are not growing, then you are dying. If you are not continuously growing and learning, then you will be left behind.

Poor people claim that they can't afford to get educated due to lack of time and money. My reply is often, "If you think education is expensive, try ignorance," which is a famous quote by Benjamin Franklin. The saying holds true that knowledge is power. Your power is in your ability to act. Most successful people are willing to learn and consistently grow their entire lives. Successful people read books, attend seminars, join masterminds, and hire consultants, because they understand that if just one new thing is learned or one improvement is made, then it's worth it. Actually, if you say that you don't have the time or the money to learn, you probably need this education the most. Using the excuse, "I don't have the money" isn't going to fly here. So, when do you think you will have the money? Maybe a year or two from now? Five years from now when you get a promotion into management? The answer is never! You will most likely be saying the same thing no matter how many years from now unless you start today and commit to being a lifelong learner.

If you want to create wealth, the only way I know for you to do that is to learn how to play the money game inside and out. You have to learn the skills and strategies to boost your income, manage the money well, and then invest the money effectively. Remember the budget from earlier in the book? Setting aside 10 percent for education can be used to buy books, audiobooks, magazines, coaching, masterminds, or anything that provides information that will propel your life forward. We all know that the definition of insanity is doing the same thing over and over and expecting a different result, so when you have a chance, take a look at if what you've been doing has been working. If it hasn't, then I trust that you know what you need to do. Whether you do it or not is a choice that only you can make!

As a coach, my goal is to train you, inspire you, encourage you, and help you achieve your goals. I'm here to hold you accountable for what you commit to do. I hate to be so in your face about it, but it's my commitment to you. I'm committed to do whatever it takes to move you to the next level in your life. You may feel like you're being ripped apart at times, but my goal is to help you become happy and a hundred times richer. If you want to move quickly and permanently, let's keep going to the end.

Success is 100 percent a learnable skill, just like anything else. If you want to be wealthy, you can learn how to do it, just like if you wanted to learn how to get into the best shape of your life or learn how to be happy. It doesn't matter where you are right now or where you were in the past. It does not matter where you are starting from or where you just came from. What matters is the willingness to learn. Here's some great news to hopefully make you feel better about the journey ahead: No one comes out of their mother's womb a financial genius. Every wealthy and successful person had to start somewhere and learn how to succeed at the money game. You can do it, too!

Becoming a financial success is not as much about the money aspect as it is about who you become in the process. You must grow in experience, character, and mind in order to get rich. The fastest path to getting rich and staying rich is to work on developing you! You are growing yourself into a "successful person." Always keep in mind that the results are the fruit and your inner world is the root. If you take care of the roots, the fruit will flourish. When you grow yourself to become a successful person who is strong in character and mind, you will be successful in anything you do! You will gain the power of choice and the ability to choose any job, business, or investment you want. You will be a success! This is the essence of this book. As you grow into a level 10 person, you will get level 10 results.

Focus on becoming a successful person on the inside and out, because if by some stroke of luck you do get rich without doing the inner work, you will most likely lose it. But by becoming successful on the inside, you will not only be happy, you will also make, keep, and grow your wealth. Financially successful people understand the order to success is BE > DO > HAVE. The poor and middle-class people believe that the order to success is HAVE > DO > BE. This is precisely why "fake it 'til you make it" doesn't work. That's why you see people with nice cars, clothes, and jewelry, but no assets. Looking successful is a lot different from actually being successful.

Most poor and middle-class people believe, "If I have a lot of money, then I can do what I want and I'd be a success." Rich people believe, "If I become a successful person, I will be able to do what I want and have what I want, including lots of money." Creating wealth is not all about the money. The goal of creating wealth is to help you grow in the absolute best version of yourself. That is the goal of all goals. Grow yourself as a person. In my opinion, success is not a "what." It is a "who." The best news I ever learned in regards to creating wealth is that who you are is 100 percent trainable and learnable. I'm speaking from my own personal experience, because by no means am I perfect or even close to it. But when I look at who I am today versus who I was 10 years ago, I can see a direct correlation between me and my wealth — or lack thereof — then and me and my wealth now. I didn't grow up in a rich family and I didn't complete college. I learned my way to success, and you can, too. I was trained to succeed, and now my goal is for you to do the same!

Another trait successful people have is that they are usually experts in their field. Just as a professional athlete, whoever is the best usually gets paid the most. The best players in every sport get paid the most. This same principle holds true in both the business and financial world. Most other people are either mediocre or not good at all in their field. Here are a few questions to ask yourself:

How good are you at what you do?

How good are you at your job?

How good are you at your business?

If you really want to know the answer to the questions above, all you have to do is look at your paycheck. That will tell you everything you need to know. If you want to get paid the best, you have to be the best. Whether you choose a salaried job, commissioned sales, start a business, network marketing, become a professional, investor, or anything else, the better you are, the more you'll earn. How do you get better? This is just another question to which the answer is by becoming a lifelong learner.

In being a lifelong learner, it's worth mentioning, rich people are sure they learn from those who have already been where they themselves want to go. The one thing that made the biggest difference for me was who I chose to learn from. I always made it a point to learn from true masters in their respective fields with real-world experience. Wealthy and successful people take advice from people who are richer than they are or at least further along in a particular area. Poor people take advice from their friends who are broke, just like them. Only take advice on a subject if you would trade places with that person.

If you decided to do a triathlon, would you hire a coach who has potato chip crumbs in his beard when you show up to train with him, or would it be smarter to find someone who has actually completed or coached someone that completed a triathlon? The obvious answer is to go with the person who has been where you are headed. I'm suggesting that you put a lot of attention and energy into being a lifelong learner, and at the same time, be selective of who you are learning and taking advice from. If you learn from those who are broke, whether consultants, coaches, or planners, they can only teach you how to do one thing: how to be broke.

I highly recommend you consider hiring a personal success and inner game coach. A good coach will keep you on track in doing what you've said you will do. Hiring performance coaches was a game changer for me. Some coaches are life coaches, who address everything, while other coaches specialize in specific areas. Some examples are personal or professional performance, finances, relationships, health, spirituality, or business. There are proven routes and strategies for creating high income, financial freedom, and wealth. You have to be willing to not only learn them, but also use them. The more you learn, the more you earn.

Millionaire Mind Shift Action Items

Commit to being a lifelong learner.

Read at least one book, audiobook, educational podcast series, or take a course/seminar each month.

Consider hiring a performance and inner game coach.

Millionaire Mind Shift #12
Create Your Life

If creating wealth is your goal, you must believe you are in the driver's seat of your financial life and your life in general. Wealthy and successful people believe that they create their life. In most cases, creating wealth will not come by a stroke of luck or your name being picked out of a hat like the lottery. If you notice, most of the people who spend a fortune playing the lottery are poor. There are many rich people who play the lottery, but not as a primary strategy to create wealth. It's usually for fun, because who wouldn't want to win the lottery, right? The difference is that they don't spend half of their paycheck on tickets.

You have to believe that you are the one who creates your success. You are also the one who creates your mediocrity. You are the one creating your struggle around money and success. It doesn't matter if you are doing it consciously or unconsciously — it's still all you. Instead of taking responsibility for what's going on in their lives, most people choose to play the role of the victim. Notice that I said they "play" the role of a victim. They are not actually victims. I don't believe that anyone is a victim. I believe that people play the role of the victim because they think it gets them something in the end. What does someone playing the role of a victim sound like?

When it comes to playing the role of a victim, most are professionals at the "blame game." The object of the blame game is to point the finger at as many people or circumstances without ever looking at yourself. Anyone who is in close proximity to victims becomes an easy target. Victims also blame the president, the government, the stock market, the housing market, the type of business they're in, their employees, the cleaning lady, God, their spouse, their partner, their manager, the other department, and of course, their parents. They are never to blame for the problem, but it's someone else or something to blame for everything in their lives.

When victims aren't blaming someone or something else, you'll overhear them justifying or rationalizing their situation by saying things like, "Having a lot of money is not important." If you told your spouse or partner that they weren't important, how long would they stick around? Not for long. The same goes for money and the creation of wealth. Would you smoke cigars if it wasn't important to you? Of course not. Would you work out and eat healthy if it wasn't important to you? Of course not. If you don't think creating wealth is important, you simply will not do it. Anyone who says money isn't important doesn't have any! Wealthy people understand the importance of money and its place in our society.

Some people will also justify things by making irrelevant comparisons like, "Money isn't more important than love." Of course, that isn't a fair comparison. Could they both be important possibly? It's like saying, "What's more important, your leg or your arm?" Well, both are important! Money is extremely important in areas where it's useful and extremely unimportant in the areas where it's not useful. Remember earlier when we discussed that money is simply a tool. A hammer cannot do what a screwdriver does, but they are both equally important in building a house. Although love is what we all need and what makes the world go 'round, it sure doesn't pay for the building and maintenance of homes, hospitals, and churches. Love doesn't feed anybody or keep the utility bill paid, either. Try going to the bank tomorrow and depositing some love.

Victims are also professional complainers. A line from one of Kanye West's songs comes to mind that says, ". . . I'm so gifted at finding what I don't like the most . . ." Victims find a problem for every solution, and nothing is ever right for them. Their food is always either undercooked or overcooked, and their drink is never mixed correctly. In my opinion, complaining is one of the worst possible things you can do for your health and wealth. I believe that whatever you focus on, you attract. When you are complaining, you're focusing on what is wrong, so you can only attract more opportunities for you to find something wrong.

Have you ever noticed how these complainers are usually living what they believe to be a "tough life"? It seems that everything that could go wrong for them, does. Their excuse is, "Of course I'm complaining, look at how awful my life is." In reality, their life seems awful because they complain about it. It's a good idea to distance yourself from complainers as much as possible. I stay away from complainers because negative energy is contagious. Many people love to hang out and listen to other complainers for one reason: They're waiting for their turn. "You think you have it bad, let me tell you how bad my life is." Discussing your problems with someone who can't help you solve them makes no sense and is a waste of time. If you've been a complainer, this is a good place to start focusing immediately. Forget about attracting for success for now, just focus on getting to neutral. By getting to neutral, you will at least stop attracting undesirable situations.

From now on, whenever you hear yourself blaming, justifying, or complaining, immediately stop yourself. Remind yourself that you create your life, and that in each moment you are either attracting success or failure. You must actively choose your thoughts and words wisely.

You may be wondering, "Who would choose to be a victim?" Being a victim definitely has its rewards. People get attention by playing the role of the victim. We all know that attention in some form or another is important and what almost everyone lives for. The main reason that people live for attention is because they are confusing attention with love. It is virtually impossible to be truly happy and successful if you're in constant need of attention. When attention is your goal, you are at the mercy of others, begging for approval. People tend to do stupid things to get attention eventually, so I recommend understanding the difference between attention and love. By disconnecting the two, you will first, be more successful, and second, be happier.

There is no such thing as a rich victim, so in order to stay a victim, attention seekers make sure to never get rich. You have to make the decision to either be rich or be a victim. You can't be both. The time for you to take back your power and acknowledge that you create everything that is in—and not in—your life is now. Read that last sentence again. You create your wealth, lack of wealth, and every level in between.

Millionaire Mind Shift Action Items

Become more self-aware and catch yourself blaming, justifying, or complaining. Stop immediately and redirect your thoughts. Decide if the thought is empowering or disempowering.

Review each day with one thing that went well and one thing that did not. Be grateful for what went well. Then ask yourself, "How did I create these situations?"

So, What Next?

I hope you enjoyed reading this book, but more importantly, I hope you use the principles to dramatically enhance your life. Although I love to read, listen to audiobooks, and learn, these things alone will not make the difference you are looking for. Reading is the start, but if you really want to succeed in the new economy, it is your actions that count. Talk is cheap. Discipline yourself to take the necessary steps even when you don't feel like it.

In Part One of this book, we discussed the concept of your money blueprint. We now know that your financial blueprint will determine your financial future. Be sure to do all of the Millionaire Mind Shift Action Items I suggested with the modeling, incidents, and verbal prompts. This will begin changing your blueprint to one that supports your financial success.

In Part Two of this book, you learned 12 specific ways in which wealthy and successful people think differently from poor and middle-class people. I recommend that you commit each of the Millionaire Mind Shifts to memory. Eventually you will find yourself viewing life—especially money—in a brand-new way. From there you will be empowered to make new choices and decisions that will, in turn, create new results for you. If you want to speed up the process, do each of the Millionaire Mind Shift Action Items at the end of each chapter. In my opinion, these action items are extremely important. Change must occur in your subconscious mind in order for it to be permanent. You are able to control your subconscious mind by feeding your conscious mind with repetition of new habits. This means you have to put the material into practice. You can't just read about it, talk about it, and just think it. You must actually do it. Resist the little voice that says, "I don't need or have time to do these action items." Don't listen to the conditioned, non-supportive files in your mind. Do the things in this book and watch your life take off!

I also suggest that you reread this book from the beginning all the way to the end at least once per month for the next year. Order the audiobook and alternate between the two if you need to. That little voice in your head may push back against this as well, saying, "I just read this book, so why would I need to find time to do it every month for a year?" That's a good question. Repetition is the mother of learning. We learn best by hearing and reading things multiple times because we undoubtedly miss something that may resonate differently each time you read. The more you study this book, the faster the concepts will become second nature for you.

I learned my way to success, and I am no more special than anyone who is reading this book. So, now it's my turn to assist others. My mission is to educate and inspire millions of people to live their best lives and be the best version of themselves. My mission is to inspire people to live based on courage and purpose versus fear, need, and obligation.

Well, that's it for now. Thank you for spending your valuable time reading this book. Be on the lookout for more books in the near future on some of the actual techniques I have used to create wealth. I did not go the traditional "financial planner route," so my path is not for everyone. I do believe that everyone should be a millionaire and be financially free, regardless of your path. I wish you tremendous success and happiness.

To Your Success,

John McNeill

www.ingramcontent.com/pod-product-compliance
Lightning Source LLC
Chambersburg PA
CBHW021414210526
45463CB00001B/371